T0322748

JOKER

THE OFFICIAL SCRIPT BOOK

THE OFFICIAL SCRIPT BOOK

SCREENPLAY BY **Todd Phillips & Scott Silver**

London

A CONVERSATION WITH
TODD PHILLIPS

JUNE 2019

Q: What are your memories of The Joker and what did you know about him before you came on to this project?

TP: I grew up not as big a comic book fan as you probably would think, having gone on to make a Joker film. But I remember always responding to the bad guys, and him in particular. I just liked his sense of mayhem and chaos. It was something that was attractive to me as a character. But he's been interpreted and done so many times over the years, and I think there hasn't been a bad one yet, so it was a little daunting.

I guess my earliest experience with The Joker was *The Killing Joke* comic. the first time I really got into him as a character in the comic books.

Q: And for yourself as a director, did you always know that you wanted to come in with this character piece? Or how did you approach that?

TP: I had never really thought about doing a comic book movie and it's not been a goal of mine. And I don't particularly watch a ton of them, although, there've been some great ones. For me it was more about this idea of, what I really hadn't done much of is a character study. And so, the idea came from, "Boy, it'd be fun to make really a singular character study."

Some of the movies I grew up on, whether it's *Serpico*, *Taxi Driver*, *King of Comedy*, *Raging Bull*, and even recently *There Will Be Blood* and *Social Network*, these are all great character study films. And I thought it would be fun to make a really good character study, but about somebody that people have no idea of who, what, where he came from. So kind of came at it that way. It wasn't like "Oh, I want to make a Joker movie." It was really came from, "How do you make a great character study and get people to want to see it?"

Q: And how did the studio react when you brought that up? Were they interested in it, or were they protective of their franchise?

TP: You know, Warner Bros. was pretty loose with it. They didn't have anything to lose in saying, "Go write it." We weren't coming to them with a finished script. I came to them, I pitched it to them as an idea first, so they don't really have anything to lose by going, "Sure, go write that. Have fun." And Scott Silver and I went off and wrote for a year, and came back with the script. But there was no rules or mandates from them. It was kind of amazing actually.

We purposely set it in the past to remove it from anything else anybody knows. And it's not really even set in the past. It's sort of set in an alternate universe in a way. It's a tough thing to explain. But they weren't really that uptight about the property. They just said, "Okay, go explore." And I met with some people at DC. Geoff Johns was running DC at the time , and he was really into the idea. And we loosely pitched him what we were thinking and then we went off and wrote it.

Q: Can you tell me a little bit about the process that you and Scott took when you came up with it and why it took you a year? What did you guys do in that year?

TP: Well, like most writing, 70 percent of writing is procrastination. So that's seven months and then you really just write. Really, no, we talked a lot about what it could be. To me, that's what writing is, you have these long conversations and long lunches where you just start talking about, "If we could do anything what would it be, and who would he be, and why is he like this, and why does he laugh?"

And what is his thing, and where does that laugh come from? And why does he wear make-up, or not? And we really just started reading a lot of, as I said, I didn't grow up on comics, but I've certainly been schooled on it since. When we were writing we did a ton of research. We watched certain movies that were definitely inspiration, like *The Man Who Laughed*, which I had seen I think in film school, but I really watched it under a different lens this time.

We read a ton of stuff about narcissism and ego and things that we think that are baked into our version of The Joker.

And it was a little bit what makes somebody this way, an exploration of that, our version of that.

Q: Can we talk a little bit about the narcissism and ego and that aspect of the psychological makeup of this guy? Because, as you said, you kind of bored in on one character.

TP: I'm not a psychoanalyst. I don't know too much about it, but I know that this idea of, The Joker is a narcissist. But he's an egoless narcissist in our mind. The ego is Arthur. The ego is the thing that's trying to control this wild horse that is The Joker. But The Joker is pure id, not to overanalyze a comic book character.

So we just thought, what happens when you go through your life wearing a mask, which a lot of people do? You're wearing a mask and you're pretending to be a certain way. And Arthur is very controlled, but there are these glimpses of who he is underneath. And whether the laugh is something that gives us a hint of that, or just the simmering anger that we feel sometimes with Arthur in the early scenes.

So there's this sort of, "What happens when you take the mask off?" Which is kind of a weird flip because actually The Joker wears a mask, or makeup. But the idea is, what happens when you stop living that life and live as the shadow? It's a Nietzschean thing with the shadow, and it's a whole thing we got into. When you ask, what did we do for that year? We did a lot of that. And then you just make the movie and you forget all that, and you just make the film and you hope it makes sense on some level.

Q: It definitely made sense.

TP: Yeah, and it's like stuff that you talk to the actors about, and you talk to Joaquin certainly about, when we're trying to find who Arthur is and who Arthur becomes, and about that transition from Arthur to The Joker. But what was really most liberating about it is that we had no rules from— you brought up from Warner Bros.—that we were able to do whatever we wanted. We really departed from a lot of the comic book things, we made up a new character, we gave him this name and we chose it out of the blue, so to speak.

And there was a real freedom in that, and I think Joaquin appreciated that, as well, of just doing our own thing.

Q: And you also got to build a new world with Scott, and you state it from the very first page that it's not Gotham City that we know cinematically, or from any other iteration on the page. Tell me a little bit about the Gotham City that you saw, and how it relates to the New York that you grew up in.

TP: We just really saw it as, even though we don't say when and where the movie takes place, in my mind it was always in New York City 1981. What did that look like and what did that feel like? And it was, from my memory of it—I mean I was only 11 or 12 years old—but my memory of it was kind of what you see in the movie. A very kind of rundown, broken-down city on every level.

And that was exciting to us, as a place to put this character, and a place to explore. It's tough when you're doing a movie, that there's been four or five interpretations of that character, so you're always inviting comparisons no matter what. Last year I produced *A Star Is Born* with Bradley Cooper. That movie had been remade four or five times. And you have to get rid of the fear of the comparisons and the expectations and all that feeling, and just go, "We're gonna just make our own thing." And yes, people in the long run are going to compare or not, or tell you this is better and this is

worse, and why this isn't good. But you just have to let all that go and create your own world, so to speak.

Q: As you guys were writing, did you have Joaquin in your mind or anyone else in your mind?

TP: Yeah. We wrote it for Joaquin. To me it was a long shot, and to Scott. We didn't know that we'd ever get Joaquin, but every time I've ever written a movie—and this is the 10th movie I've written, I think—I always have to write it with an

actor in mind or a personality in mind. Oftentimes you don't end up getting that person, but it really helps fuel the writing.

I don't know how else to explain it. But we really specifically wrote for Joaquin. What does that mean? He's not a particular thing, he's done so many varied things, but it was the person we were seeing when we would talk about it, and then when we were done it just became "Ugh, how are going to get this guy? And what if we don't?"

Q: What did you want out of your lead that made you think of Joaquin? You've mentioned that you thought of some of the Paul Thomas Anderson movies, his great character studies. I'm curious if that stuck with you.

TP: Yeah, certainly his previous works stuck with me. But really what I like about Joaquin is his style and his unpredictability, which it felt very much fits into this character. He's playing jazz while other people are doing math. He's just doing his own thing, and I feel like that's very much what we saw the character of Arthur/The Joker as.

He's just such a unique actor. Anybody who makes movies, whether they like or don't like the movies he's been in, everyone thinks he's one of the greatest. And I just thought, boy, if we get him we could really do something special.

Q: How did you get him?

TP: That was a difficult process. That's just like getting any actor, although probably he's a little more difficult. The standard thing is, you send the thing to his agent, or a letter to him ...and he was open, and I started going up to his house and then, going up to his house more and just talking. We would have these long conversations about it. He had the script, he liked the script, but he had certainly had a ton of questions.

And I think he also had the same thing I have, which is this fear of this is a big thing to take on, this isn't going to be a small little anonymous film no matter how it ends up. So there's a certain fear. I love that fear. I kind of had turned it into adrenaline, and you just go and make the movie. But I think a lot of it was just us talking through that stuff, and then I'm sure he had his own reservations about having never worked with me and all these other things. It just becomes a process of getting to know each other. And I think we spent a few months doing that before he said he would do it.

Q: And did you notice, as you guys started talking, that he fell further and further into the character?

TP: We never rehearsed the character. We never talked really specifically about what he would do. He is somebody that has to do it in the moment, and feel it, and get into it on his own a little bit. Certainly he would do things and we would talk, but all we really talked about was script and story and character. We never talked about "How are you going to do it?" I think his process is one of surprise for himself, not that he's holding it back and he wants to surprise me. I think some of it is, just it coming in to him. I hate to talk about people's process because I don't even know that that's it, and maybe he'll kind of clarify that better. But standing away from it, looking back on it, that seems to be part of his thing.

Q: Well, let's talk about Arthur's character a little bit since that's something you guys dwelled on a lot. Who is this guy, Arthur Fleck? Where is he in the world when we run into him, and what do we catch in terms of his transformation to this other character?

TP: I think he's an outcast in some regards, and he's a person who could use a little empathy in a world that didn't have a lot of empathy for him, and there are parallels you can make with now, and those certainly aren't necessarily coincidences. But what does it feel like to be somebody like that in a world that lacks empathy? And so, specifically, he's damaged.

We're not really sure why. How do you treat somebody like that? Well, you can ignore it, or you can actually treat them with kindness and empathy, and try to help when you can or

JOAQUIN PHOENIX
JOKER
PUT ON A HAPPY FACE
PUT ON A HAPPY FACE
JOKER

where you can. But nobody seems to do that with him, and that's kind of the story that we landed on.

Q: And he is living with his mother and they have a complicated story as well. Can you tell me about his relationship with Penny and how that has affected his daily life?

TP: Well, his relationship with Penny is in his mind, fairly standard. I don't think he really knows exactly his history with his mother, who may or may not be his mom, which we discover or not. He's a guy who's been in and out of institutions his whole life, and when he's out he probably stays with his mom and she probably wishes he would get on his feet and have his own life, but he doesn't. I think he has a not-so-complicated relationship with his mom, until it becomes complicated.

Q: He seems the most at ease when he's with her, when he's quote-unquote, "Happy."

TP: Yeah, it seems to be that's when he's able take that mask off, halfway at least, with his mom.

Q: And how about what he's up to? He's working as a kind of clown-for-hire. What's going on there?

TP: He works at a company called Ha-Ha's, which is where they rent out talent for parties, whether it's a magician or a male stripper for a bachelorette party or clowns for birthday parties. He works for a guy named Hoyt who has this sort of business that was handed down from his dad. This is all backstory, it's not necessarily in the movie. Hoyt runs this company, Ha-Ha's, where he basically is a talent agent for party entertainment. And Arthur just one of the clowns that works there.

Q: Is he a good clown?

TP: I think he's pretty good at his job. It's an odd job for him to choose, in a weird way. The movie starts with him in the mirror and he's doing this happy face and sad face thing, and it's really Arthur quite literally staring at himself deciding, is my life really the tragedy I think it is? Maybe my life is a comedy. Where is my place in this? And then we learn as it goes on.

Q: He does mention that line later on that he had thought of his life as a tragedy, but he realizes it's a comedy. Tell me a little bit about that line, and what it meant for you guys building a tragedy where he sees it as a comedy.

TP: It has a lot to do with him being just out of step of the world, and that's how while we believe the movie is a tragedy, he sees it as a comedy. And I think that is very indicative of who The Joker is, because he sees comedy in the tragedy. Which a lot of people do to some extent, but maybe not to that extent. Yeah, I think it's really one of the most important lines in the movie. And the movie opens sort of foreshadowing that.

Q: We talked a little bit about the New York that you know. But I just wanted to ask you a little bit more about the Gotham City that you built, and the kind of state that it's in when we jump in on the movie. There's a trash strike going on, social services are being canceled left and right, it's not the best place to be, especially if you're down and out like Arthur and his family. Tell me about that aspect of the powder keg of the city, and how that plays in your story.

TP: I think a lot of the movie works because there's tension, really you feel it with everything that Joaquin does in the movie and on set. He brings a level of tension to the film. But we also bring that tension in other ways, whether it's score or production design, or setting, and so we thought it was really important that the city feels it's on the edge. Like you say, a powder keg. And so when we introduce the city, which is a character in the movie—settings often are—it is on the brink. It was that time in New York, remember on the cover of the *New York Post*? "Ford To City: Drop Dead." It's that version of Gotham City. It's rundown. We're in the midst of a trash strike. I think they're six weeks into a trash strike.

Social services are being cut, which affects people like Arthur, and there's a guy running for mayor who doesn't seem to be the best guy to be mayor at that point in the city. He doesn't seem... maybe he lacks empathy.

So yeah, that's the Gotham City that we built. Mark Friedberg, our production designer, I think he did some amazing work in so many practical locations. We shot all over the Bronx and Brooklyn, and we shot a little bit in Newark, New Jersey, bringing Gotham City to life, and Mark Friedberg, he just crushed it on every level.

Q: He's a fellow New Yorker, too, right?

TP: Yeah.

Q: He just seemed to have fun kind of finding corners of the city that hadn't been seen on screen.

TP: It's hard, New York's been shot so much. But even when they were in a place that has been shot, we're making it look unique to our Gotham City. Mark grew up on the Upper West Side his whole life, he remembers—he's a few years older than me, remembers 1981 New York as a very specific time. So I think he had a lot of fun with that.

Q: And you have a long-standing collaboration with Larry Sher in terms of shooting films. You were able to make New York, Gotham City, whatever you want to call it, look pretty wonderful with him. What about his contribution?

TP: You have a lot of partners when you make a movie. When you start the movie, my partner is Scott Silver, and we write the movie. When you make the movie, my partner is Larry Sher. I think this is our sixth or seventh film—and we start talking really early, and Larry is involved in a lot of location scouting early, obviously, but I even run casting by Larry.

I get his opinion on a ton of stuff that isn't necessarily just DP-oriented stuff, because we've just made a lot of movies together. I love his taste. He has the best eye of anybody that I know, so I really have a lot of trust in Larry and it just—it just helps on every level.

Q: What do you like about how your movie looks, thanks to Larry?

TP: I think the movie looks great for...I think it's what we set out to make. We started looking at a lot of movies together that took place back then in New York. And we just tried to not mimic those movies, but movies are such a great time capsule. You know, you watch *Dog Day Afternoon*. They didn't art direct that, meaning the street was the street and you go, "Oh, look. It's a great time capsule," what New York looked like in 1976.

So you start watching those movies together with Mark Friedberg, and Mark Bridges the costume designer, and Larry, and we start talking about the color palette and all that stuff. Larry, he's just a great shooter so he brings so much. It's hard to kind of put it in a sentence what Larry brings, or Mark Bridges, or Mark Friedberg, but it's a lot.

Q: Of course. And it's always the worst question to ask about a DP...the only one harder than that is asking about someone's editor.

TP: Yeah. Well, that's the third collaborator. So I said that you have the first collaborator is the writer, my co-writer. The second is Larry when we're making the movie. And then the third is Jeff Groth, who's the editor who edited my last couple of movies. The best way to describe what an editor does is, it's the final rewrite. You're literally rewriting the movie again in the editing room. So I look at editors as writers, or co-writers in that room, and you just have to be to be open-minded to explore, and really put the script away. That's old news, now let's see what we have. And things might get rejiggered a ton. So Jeff's been a great collaborator.

Q: For sure. You talked a tiny bit about casting. Building a world around Joaquin was complicated as well. Tell me who you brought in and what you liked about their performances.

TP: Well, you know, the movie is 95 percent Joaquin Phoenix. I mean it; when I say it's a character study, he's in every scene in the film, and if you're not a Joaquin Phoenix fan you should just avoid the movie altogether because he is in every frame. So then to build it around him, I wanted to surround him with great actors, like every director does. I would say that the biggest other role in the movie is the Robert De Niro role, because he has the biggest scenes with Joaquin.

And then there's Zazie Beetz and Frances Conroy. And then Brett Cullen, who plays Thomas Wayne. There are a lot of other actors in the movie, but I think those were the four key ones to focus on. And De Niro, he's Robert De Niro. He's the greatest of all time. I mean literally. So we aimed high and we went to him first and he loved the script...and he got it. He got what it meant. And we got on the phone and we talked. And then I think I met him in New York, and that went pretty quickly and pretty easily. None of these other actors had a huge time commitment, so that always works in your favor: "Okay, Bob, I know it's not a giant role, but it's going to take two weeks and we can do it in September." And so that helps also. He just really loved the idea of working with Joaquin. Joaquin and I were thrilled. Joaquin is probably a bigger De Niro fan than I am even. It meant a lot. And then with Frances... I don't really remember the process. I remember meeting Frances for coffee and talking to her about it. And Zazie came in. We had auditioned a few girls for that part. Zazie came in and read with Joaquin and was fantastic. We loved her, and it sort of was traditional casting.

Q: When it came to De Niro you did mention making *Comedy* and *Taxi Driver*.

TP: Yeah

Q: And in a way I'm just curious as to your thoughts there. When I saw the movie those things melted away for me.

TP: Yeah.

Q: But I saw it in the script really thoroughly.

TP: Yeah. One of my favorite movies as a kid was *King of Comedy*. I just think that is, tonally, such a weird movie. Like the way they handled tone in that film is kind of a case study in tone. Nobody ever understands what tone is. And as you watch that movie and you go, oh, that's like a case study in tonality in movies. I just love that movie, and so when we were writing it there's clearly a little bit of a parallel with the talk show. So Scott Silver and I, when we were writing it were

thinking, boy, wouldn't it be unbelievable if we got to De Niro, who played Rupert Pupkin in that movie—not the talk show host—to play the talk show host in this film? Bob got it on the first bounce when he read the script and understood it. And there's a special place, I think, in his heart for that film as well. Even though it's not one of his more well-known movies, it's just phenomenal. A lot of people don't even know that movie. But for the people that do, we just thought that would be a cool thing.

Q: It's amazing that that movie would be lost to history somehow.

TP: I don't know that it's lost, but it certainly you have to be a somewhat of a film buff to know it. I mean it's not that obscure, but a lot of people I know haven't seen it.

Q: Can you talk a little bit about Arthur's aspiration to be a comedian, and that sliver of hope that he has, and it how might perhaps save him from becoming what he becomes?

TP: Well, Arthur has this affliction where he laughs and it's almost like Tourette's, but the laugh can go on for a minute and a half. And it's just comes out of nowhere and has nothing to do with how he feels or who he's with. It's just something that comes on. It might come on a little bit from nerves. It might come on from a tense situation, but it often comes at inappropriate times. So he's had that his whole life. His mother told him he was born laughing, which we learn isn't really true. And it may be that something that she did, or something that she didn't do, had something to do with that laugh being developed.

But he was told as a child, his whole life, that he was born laughing. She calls him Happy as a nickname, as a loving nickname to him because of that laugh. And she's explained to him over the years that this is your purpose in life, to bring joy and laughter to the world. So he's growing up thinking that, and I think that's what's led him into the life of wanting to be a standup comedian, of being a clown, a performer. All those things kind of led him down that path.

But he wasn't necessarily cut out for it.

Q: No, his book is not exactly the funniest book you've ever read.

TP: Yeah, it's funny to me and Joaquin but most people would think it's not. He wasn't on the path of Jerry Seinfeld. I think he got some bad advice at a young age from his mom. He probably wasn't cut out to be a clown or a comedian.

Q: Can you tell me a little bit about Arthur's joke book. It's a special little prop of his.

TP: He keeps this journal. We learn early on in the movie that Arthur goes to a probably court-mandated social worker, where he has to check in every couple of weeks. And I think it was her idea to have him start a journal. Arthur keeps it as a semi-journal, but also as a joke book where he makes, as he puts it, funny thoughts or observations he has during the day. They're not particularly funny or insightful.

But I shouldn't say that. They are insightful into who he is, and where his mind goes. But it's just a device we used in the screenplay as something that is another one of those things I was talking about, that keep him in check so to speak. And when he lets go of the journal and he lets go of Arthur, and he just lives as the wild horse and he's pure id, that's where he's let go of all the reins.

Q: It does make sense. There is an amazing moment after he commits his first really gruesome violence in the subway, where he finds his way into a bathroom and achieves this weird state of grace through movement. I don't even remember, is that on the pages? Is that something that just developed?

TP: That developed, and one of the things about working with somebody like Joaquin Phoenix. And what was so exciting to me about it is, you know, to work with somebody like that you have to be incredibly nimble as a director. And I knew that just from the meetings I had with him at his house. I knew that from talking to other directors. And through doing comedies before this... you have to be nimble, too. There's so

much that comes up on a comedy that is spur of the moment, whether it's improvisation or just "It'd be really funny if we do this." And you throw a wrench in the whole thing, and you do it because you're servicing the joke. Well, working with Joaquin, it wasn't all that different, and you needed to be facile. So we got to that set. That was a set and you know, in the script it was very... oh, we had scripted a scene where Arthur runs into the bathroom and he has to get rid of this gun that he had been given, that was now evidence.

And what was in the script was, he pulls the grate off the bathroom wall, and he hides his gun in there. And then he kind of washes his face, the make-up off his face and all this stuff. And when we got in the bathroom that day, it was just me and Joaquin and we're standing there. We're kind of "Eh, we should put it in this grate." And we just start talking about, does Arthur really care about evidence? And does Arthur really care about...does he even know enough? Like, what, did he see this in a movie, "hide a gun?" Why is it even in his language to do that?

And then we're like, yeah, let's not do that. Okay. Well, what should we do? And then we just started talking about things we could do in that bathroom, on that day of shooting, that would express the sort of change that he went through. And hiding the gun seemed very practical for this impractical guy. And I think we were literally in there for an hour just figuring out what to do. And we were at a standstill. We hadn't really figured it out and I said, "Oh, you know, I got this great piece of music I want to play you." From the composer — another collaborator on a movie that is integral and so important. So I said, "I want to play this piece of music I just got from Hildur [Guðnadóttir]. I think it's great, and I've just been listening to it all night. She sent it to me yesterday." And so I played it for him and he loved it, and he just started doing this dance to it. And he just kept doing it and I said, "Maybe this is what it is," and we started working that out.

And then I called in Geoff Haley, the camera operator, and we just started shooting it. I think it's a really great moment in the movie. And it's a really much more effective way of illustrating the beginning of a transformation. And like you said, with grace that kind of comes out of nowhere, you kind of feel that he has it in him. You know, we wrote in the script there's a certain elegance to him and a certain romance. And when he holds the door for the women and he puts his foot out with a little bit of air, the way he dances in the beginning of the film as a clown, he has it in him. There's music in him so to speak. But that's the first time we really see it come out.

Q: And then as time goes on and he settles into himself a little bit more, the movement and the dance becomes more a part of his personality.

TP: Yeah, it does. And it's that the shadow that starts to take over and become the thing. And that's really what's happening in that. It's the first emergence of this kind of shadow.

Q: It's interesting that you compared it to *Comedy* because, from your experience having worked for so long on comedies, coming around to this tragedy—or however you want to describe it—I just was curious about your reaction to the form, and to the genre, and trying to figure that out and piece it together. But seeing this improv within it, it seems like you have some similar elements.

TP: Yeah, I do. And, you know, I'm surprised when people— and it's never people that make movies. It's always other people that say "Well, he does comedies. He doesn't do that." And to me, it's always been storytelling. I mean I actually started making movies, I made three documentaries before I made comedies, and I didn't even see that as a leap. It's just storytelling. It just always comes down to a beginning, middle, and end. Telling a story that you hope people will be engaged in. And tonally, I think if you watch some of my comedies, they're always a little bit darker than your standard studio comedies. So it was always there. We just kept kind of stepping closer and closer to that.

Q: For sure. I mean when you brought up *The King of Comedy* as a tonal study, that's a really dark, nasty movie.

TP: Yeah, it was the greatest.

Q: If you just describe what happened to someone they'd be like, well, that's a horrible story.

TP: Right. Right.

Q: But it's the funniest movie ever.

TP: Yeah. It really is.

Q: So you mentioned early on that Joaquin surprised you all the time, and probably surprised himself, which is equally interesting. Did you find that he was someone who would let himself be open to performance through the shoot?

TP: Oh, my God, yeah. I think he is the most—talk about nimble—nimble actor I've ever worked with, certainly. He just doesn't get stuck in anything. He will try. I mean we've been editing this movie for so long because there's I think 18 trillion versions of this movie just based on the way he would do things so differently every time. You would come over to him and give him one line of direction, and it would literally change everything in a great way. And he was just never locked into one thing. We never had this conversation, but I think what he appreciated about me in the long run was, as a director I wasn't locked in either. And I really kept the experience alive for him, which was able to keep him in that space. He was living in a kind of dark space that Arthur had, but I think the idea that anything could happen every day helped fuel him in a way.

Q: Did he surprise you with his transformation of his body by the time he showed up for day one?

TP: Well, it didn't surprise me because I saw him a lot over that time. So we talked a lot about, oh, how skinny should The Joker, should Arthur, be, and how far do we want to go? It surprised me the way he does it, because I've known actors for a long time now, and they get a doctor and a nutritionist. And I kept saying to him, "When are you gonna start losing weight? At what point do you start this?" Because it was already like June and he hadn't started and we start shooting in September, and he's like 180 pounds—which, he wasn't fat.

But we're talking about getting to 125 pounds. And he goes, "Ah, I got it. I got it. I got." And I go, "Well, you know, we can hire a guy, this woman is a nutritionist, you might wanna..." "No. No. No, that's not how I do it." I go, "How do you do it?" He goes, "I just stop eating and I starve myself." And starting on June 1st— and we started shooting September 12th—he just ate an apple a day for the whole summer. He would just basically eat an apple a day, and it's so unhealthy a way to do it and he knows it. He just can't do it any other way. He is, I think, one of the great procrastinators in that way.

Q: But it worked.

TP: Yeah, I know it worked. Whatever your method, I think you could have done it in a more healthy way, but that's on him. But yeah, he just stopped eating.

Q: You mentioned Mark Bridges a little bit as well, and I'm curious. You had a few iconic things that you played off of, in terms of his end look; same with make-up and hair. But you guys made something original out of it and I'm just curious about, how Joaquin got to that place that he needed to get to physically. And in another regard, you dressed him with some homage to the character but in other ways very originally. Tell me a little bit about how that final look developed.

TP: I know having spoken to many actors, I think nothing helps them more than wardrobe, weirdly. But I get it. Even walking into Arthur's apartment for the first time for Joaquin, I don't think has the same effect as putting on the clothing. I really think putting on that skin, so to speak, helps actors that final step in.

Mark Bridges is one of the best costume designers working in movies. He's won two Academy Awards. He's big time. I never

worked with him before. I wrote him a letter and sent him the script. And we went and had breakfast and met. He loved the script. He knew Joaquin. He had done *The Master* and *Inherent Vice* with Joaquin. And he was interested and excited and we just started from that day talking about, you know, what the look is. And what does Arthur dress as, and how drab is too drab? And we kind of want him to be anonymous, but not so. And we were talking, of course, about The Joker look which is so important to so many fans and people and so iconic. And in every version that The Joker has been, you can imagine their wardrobes. We wanted to do the something different but similar—it's just a lot of discussions. And Mark comes with fabrics and colors. And we talk about, this suit that he wears on stage at the comedy club is actually the same suit that he is as The Joker.

But we kind of subtly change the tone of the fabric and hope you don't really notice. It's really always that same suit, he has one suit. He's not a guy that would have five suits, right? And, of course Joaquin is involved in that. It's not something Mark and I do off in a corner. And we meet and we try things on and I love that part of it. Weirdly, I like prep in a movie because you're making so many big decisions that will live. Whether it's the color green of his hair and the look of the make-up, which is tremendous, you're making these giant decisions in prep that are going to live for a long time.

Q: Can you tell me about his final makeup and hair, and the clown face that you guys came in with at the end?

TP: Again, and it maybe to the chagrin of true comic book fans , we just wanted to make something that felt grounded in a reality. We didn't see dropping Arthur Fleck into a vat of acid and turning him white. That wasn't the movie we're making. That's amazing for The Joker's origin or how he got that in the comic books. But we just want to try something that felt a little bit more grounded in reality. We thought, well, he's a clown anyway. He has his clown makeup, maybe that's part of the thing. The idea of clowns taking over Gotham City became a theme in the movie, so it all kind of tied in.

As far as the final look, you know, Nicki [Ledermann] and Kay [Georgiou] had a ton to do with it. And Hugh [Sicotte]...he does a lot of our concept drawings. Hugh actually started doing the concept drawings for me before we even hired hair and makeup, and we started playing with the look of The Joker. Then when I hired Kay and Nicki, we looked at Hugh's drawings and that was at least a launching off point.

Q: And speaking of comic book fans, there are no superheroes in your movie at all. I think that's the big expectation, and you manage to pull it off without that, no Batman ever appeared.

TP: Yeah, there is no Batman. Nobody flies. There's not a lot of action in the movie. We really wanted to make a true character study and you know, while it might not be for everyone, we just thought that was an interesting approach.

The thing about the movie is, there's many ways to look at the movie. He might not be The Joker or Arthur. I mean one thing that I remember from *The Killing Joke*, the thing that stands out is when he says his past has always been multiple choice. I'm paraphrasing. And I think some people will come into this movie and, this is just a version of a The Joker origin. It's the version this guy is telling in this room at a mental institution. I don't know that he's the most reliable narrator in the world.

Q: Right. I think it's interesting and it's amazing that DC, the studio, and you guys are willing to play with it that way. And it doesn't have to tie in to nineteen other movies.

TP: Yeah, I mean it feels, DC feels like they're at an interesting place where they're able to do...listen, nothing is ever going to be more successful than Marvel. But in some respects, because you're not Marvel, you can fuck around with the format a little bit more. You can do things that they can't do. And that was kind of my pitch for it.

Q: It's interesting to see this pillar of society, the Wayne family, from the other side, not as the villain, but just, as you said it, not an empathetic character.

TP: Yeah. And I've just loved bad guys. And I always wonder, it's fun to say, "Well why is he like that? What made him like that?" And that's ultimately really the goal of the movie. It's not this gigantic statement on the world today. Really it's, "What makes somebody that way? And why does the bad guys have to die in the end?" I don't like that. I wanted Scarface to live forever.

Q: What we see in the end, he's in Arkham but it's a kind of a weird elegiac. It's an odd ending, the long take in the hallway. It ends on a poetic note as opposed to a hard note.

TP: Here's a guy who always thought his life was a tragedy, but it's a comedy. And we just thought in some ways... a little bit like a comedy but like an old-timey comedy. There's a little bit of like Chaplinesque stuff running through Arthur. I'm not saying the movie verges on that. I wouldn't compare it at all ever to something like that. But there's a little Chaplin, there's a little music in Arthur and that ending is sort reflective of that.

Q: Has this movie surprised you?

TP: Has the movie surprised me? Yeah, but every movie surprises me, because you start out with one idea and it takes on a life of its own. And that happens through so many facets; through the actors, through production, through things not working the way they're supposed to work, through scenes not coming together the way you thought they were going to come together. So yeah, the movie has surprised me [a] zillion times. But that's not exclusive to this movie, I would say.

Q: What do you like about this movie at this stage?

TP: I think what I like about the movie most is the boldness of the idea; taking something and taking a genre like this and really trying to do something bold and out of step with what everybody else is doing in that genre. I think ideally that's what audiences will respond to. It's not just that it's called *Joker*, it's "Oh, yeah, you're trying something different." And I just think that's always exciting.

JOKER
an origin

written by

Todd Phillips & Scott Silver

1 DECEMBER 2018

FINAL SHOOTING SCRIPT

This story takes place in its own universe. It has no connection to any of the DC films that have come before it.

We see it as a classic Warner Bros. movie. Gritty, intimate, and oddly funny, the characters live in the real world and the stakes are personal.

Although it is never mentioned in the film, this story takes place in the past.

Let's call it 1981.

It's a troubled time. The crime rate in Gotham is at record highs. A garbage strike has crippled the city for the past six weeks. And the divide between the "haves" and the "have-nots" is palpable. Dreams are beyond reach, slipping into delusions.

TP/SS

OVER BLACK:

HEAR LAUGHTER.

The sound of a man totally cracking up.

FADE IN:

INT. DEPT. OF HEALTH, OFFICE—MORNING

CLOSE ON ARTHUR (30s), tears in his eyes from laughing so hard. He's trying to get it under control. His greasy, black hair hanging down over his forehead. He's wearing an old, faded green cardigan sweater, a threadbare gray scarf, thin from years of use, hangs loosely around his neck.

He's sitting across from an overworked SOCIAL WORKER (50s), African American. Her office is cramped and run-down in a cramped and run-down building. Stacks of folders piled high in front of her.

She just sits behind her desk, waiting for his laughing fit to end, she's been through this before. Finally it subsides.

Arthur takes a deep breath, pauses to see if it's over. Beat.

> ARTHUR
> —is it just me, or is it getting crazier out there?

Despite the laughter, there's real pain in his eyes.

Something broken in him. Looks like he hasn't slept in days.

Beat.

> SOCIAL WORKER
> It's certainly tense. People are upset, they're struggling. Looking for work. The garbage strike seems like it's been going on forever. These are tough times.
>
> (then)
>
> How 'bout you. Have you been keeping up with your journal?

> ARTHUR
> Everyday.

> SOCIAL WORKER
> Great. Did you bring it with you?

Beat.

ARTHUR
(dodging the subject)
I'm sorry. Did I bring what?

SOCIAL WORKER
(impatient; she doesn't have time for this)
Arthur, last time I asked you to
bring your journal with you.
For these appointments. Do you
have it?

ARTHUR
Yes ma'am.

Beat.

SOCIAL WORKER
Can I see it?

He reluctantly reaches into the pocket of his jacket hanging
on the chair behind him. Pulls out a weathered notebook.
Slides it across to her—

ARTHUR
I've been using it as a journal,
but also a joke diary. Funny
thoughts or, or observations—
Did I tell you I'm pursuing a
career in stand-up comedy?

She's half-listening as she flips through his journal.

SOCIAL WORKER
No. You didn't.

ARTHUR

I think I did.

She doesn't respond, keeps flipping through his journal—

PAGES AND PAGES OF NOTES, neat, angry-looking handwriting. Also, cut out photos from hardcore pornographic magazines and some crude handmade drawings.

A flash of anger crosses Arthur's face—

ARTHUR

I didn't realize you wanted to
read it.

The social worker gives him a look, then reads something in the pages that gives her pause—

SOCIAL WORKER
(reading out loud)
"I just hope my death makes
more sense than my life."

She looks up at Arthur. He just stares back. Lets it hang out there for a beat.

Then he laughs a little, even though he doesn't think it's funny—

ARTHUR
Yeah. I mean, that's just—

SOCIAL WORKER
Does my reading it upset you?

He leans in.

> **ARTHUR**
> No. I just,—some of it's personal.
> You know?

> **SOCIAL WORKER**
> I understand. I just want to
> make sure you're keeping up
> with it.

She slides his journal back to him. He holds it in his lap.

> **SOCIAL WORKER**
> How does it feel to have to come
> here? Does it help having
> someone to talk to?

> **ARTHUR**
> I think I felt better when I was
> locked up, in the hospital.

> **SOCIAL WORKER**
> And have you thought more
> about why you were "locked
> up?"

> **ARTHUR**
> Well I suppose I was mentally ill.

> **SOCIAL WORKER**
> How's that?

> **ARTHUR**
> Well my mother thought I was
> mentally ill, so she had me
> committed.

> SOCIAL WORKER
> Did you *feel* mentally ill?

> ARTHUR
> They've been saying that since I
> was little. So who knows.

Long pause.

> ARTHUR
> I was wondering if you could
> ask the doctor to increase my
> medication.

The social worker ruffles through some papers—

Beat.

> SOCIAL WORKER
> Arthur, you're on seven
> different medications. Surely
> they must be doing something.

> ARTHUR
> I just don't want to feel so bad
> anymore.

And we HEAR "TEMPTATION RAG" playing on a broken
down piano—

**EXT. GOTHAM SQUARE, MIDTOWN—AFTERNOON—DAYS
LATER**

CLOSE ON ARTHUR, NOW DRESSED UP AS A CLOWN,
painted white face... Wide red smile outlined in black around
his mouth... Bulbous red nose... Bald cap with two patches of
frizzy green hair sticking out over the ears, little bowler hat...

Too-tight buttoned jacket... Baggy pants and oversized colored shoes. This is his job.

PULLING OUT, we see he's holding a sign in front of Kenny's Music Shop that reads, "EVERYTHING MUST GO!" A banner above the store reads, "GOING OUT OF BUSINESS!" Behind him, an OLD MAN plays an old piano on the busy street, garbage bags piled everywhere.

Arthur's doing a little Charlie Chaplin like performance to the music, twirling the sign, bringing attention to the sale. He's pretty good, feeling the music in his bones, light on his feet. Still most people walk right past, ignoring him.

ARTHUR SEES A GROUP OF BOYS pointing at him from down the street, laughing at him... One of the boys throws an empty Coke can at Arthur as they get close... Arthur holds up the sign like a shield, Coke can bouncing off it—

The boys walk up on Arthur... He tries ignoring them, keeps dancing to the old ragtime, holding up the sign as they surround him... One of the kids knocks the sign out of Arthur's hands—

The other kids crack up. Arthur bends over to pick up his sign and... Kicks it... Attempts to pick it up again and... Kicks it again... It's a bit.

Arthur bends over a third time to pick up the sign and... One of the boys kicks him right in the ass—

Arthur falls face first onto the sidewalk. Oddly, the old man playing the piano picks up the pace of the music—

The kids crack up. One of the boys grabs Arthur's sign and takes off running across the street—

The other kids follow, weaving through traffic—

Arthur gets up and gives chase. He needs his sign back.

He almost gets hit by a taxi, spinning out of the way just in time—Spinning right into another taxi that stops just short of hitting him.

Arthur keeps running through traffic. People stare. A clown barreling down the street has got to be a joke—

EXT. CORNER, ALLEY—GOTHAM SQUARE—CONTINUOUS

The five boys are booking it down the busy street laughing and whooping it up. At the last second they take a sharp right turn down an alley—

Arthur almost overshoots the corner, slip-sliding in his oversized shoes—

He rights himself and heads down after them—Sees them running up ahead—*WHAP!* Out of nowhere Arthur gets hit in the face! He falls to the ground.

One of the kids was hiding behind a dumpster and hit Arthur with the "EVERYTHING MUST GO!" sign, splintering it in two—

The other kids turn back and walk up to Arthur down on the ground.

Arthur reaches out, still trying to save the sign—

THE KIDS START KICKING AND BEATING THE SHIT out of Arthur. It's brutal and vicious. Nobody on the street stops to help.

CLOSE ON ARTHUR'S CLOWN FACE, down on the ground. Sweat running down his face, smearing his makeup. Doesn't even look like he's in pain. He just takes the beating. Arthur's good at taking a beating.

That stupid smile painted on his face.

TITLE:

JOKER

INT. CITY BUS (MOVING)—HEADING UPTOWN—LATE AFTERNOON

Arthur sitting in the back of a crowded bus, looking out the window at the city passing him by... his makeup's washed off, still see some white grease-paint smudged on the sides of his face.

He feels somebody staring, turns to see a sad-eyed THREE-YEAR-OLD BOY, face puffy from crying, sitting on his knees looking back at him. His mother's facing forward, but even from behind you can tell she's angry.

Arthur doesn't know where to look, feeling self-conscious and small. He gets back into "character" smiling like a clown and covers his face with his hands—Starts playing the peek-a-boo game with him.

The boy stares back at him for a moment then giggles—

>   WOMAN ON BUS
>   (turns back to Arthur; already annoyed)
>   Can you please stop bothering
>   my kid?

>   ARTHUR
>   I wasn't bothering him, I was—

>   WOMAN ON BUS
>   (interrupts)
>   Just stop.

AND SUDDENLY ARTHUR STARTS TO LAUGH. LOUD. He covers his mouth trying to hide it—Shakes his head, laughter pausing for a moment, but then it comes on stronger. His eyes are sad. It actually looks like the laughter causes him pain.

People on the bus are staring. The little boy looks like he's going to cry again.

>   WOMAN ON BUS
>   You think that's funny?

Arthur shakes his head no, but he can't stop laughing. He reaches in his pocket and pulls out a small card. Hands it to the woman.

CLOSE ON THE CARD, it reads: "Forgive my laughter. I have a condition (more on back)"

She turns the card over and there is a bunch of information in small writing—

"It's a medical condition causing sudden, frequent, uncontrollable laughter that doesn't match how you feel. It can happen in people with a brain injury or certain neurological conditions."

She doesn't read it (but if you freeze frame the movie you could). She just shakes her head annoyed and throws the card on the ground.

Arthur laughs harder. Tears running down his face.

Not wanting to attract any more attention to himself, he covers his mouth with his threadbare scarf, trying to muffle the laughter—

EXT. THE BRONX, STREET—SUNSET

The bus pulls away, sun almost gone.

Arthur heads slowly limping down the litter-covered streets. Garbage is piled along the sidewalks, the air thick with smog creates a haze over everything.

The streets are crowded with the poor, the elderly, and disenfranchised. Women with children in busted strollers. Homeless people sleeping on subway grates. Stray dogs. His is one of the few white faces.

Arthur makes his way into a run-down drug store, behind him two drunks fight on the corner, beating the shit out of each other. Arthur, and nobody else for that matter, pays them any attention.

No one here gives a shit.

EXT. SIDE ALLEY, TENEMENTS—EARLY DUSK

Arthur cuts through a garbage filled alley behind decaying apartment buildings. Holding a small white (prescription) bag in his hand. Tenants overhead leaning out their windows, smoking out their windows, laughing, arguing over loud music.

A BUNCH OF YOUNG KIDS HANGING OUT ON A FIRE ESCAPE, yell down at Arthur giving him shit in Spanish.

EXT. STEEP STAIRWAY, TENEMENTS—DUSK

Arthur turns from the street, looking up at a long, steep concrete stairway that seems to go up forever, cutting between two tenement buildings, graffiti tags sprayed all over the brick walls. He starts the long climb up, step-after-step-after-step-after-step...

INT. APARTMENT BUILDING, LOBBY—DUSK

A shabby lobby in a building that was once probably pretty nice, but now it's a dump.

Arthur checks his mailbox. He's still holding the small white bag in his hand.

The mailbox is empty.

INT. ELEVATOR, APARTMENT BUILDING—CONTINUOUS

Arthur steps onto the small, graffiti-covered elevator, flickering fluorescent lights.

INT. MOM'S APARTMENT, FRONT DOOR—EVENING

Old apartment, worn carpet. Nothing's new inside but it's fairly neat and well-kept.

> PENNY (OS)
> (shattering the moment)
> Happy?! Did you check the mail
> before you came up?

> ARTHUR
> Yes, Ma. Nothing. No letter.

His mother, PENNY FLECK (60s), comes in all made up. She walks over and gives him a kiss on the cheek. He covers the pain from his beating the best he can—His mother doesn't seem to notice anyway.

PENNY

You sure you looked?
Sometimes I don't know where
your head is.

ARTHUR

Yes I'm sure. And my head's right
here. Go lie down, I'm gonna
make you some dinner, okay?

QUICK CUTS:

ARTHUR TEARS OPEN THE PRESCRIPTION BAG... A FLURRY
OF PILL BOTTLES TUMBLE OUT ONTO THE COUNTER.

SEE HIS NAME, "ARTHUR FLECK" ON THE ORANGE PILL
BOTTLES, TEMAZEPAM... PERPHENAZINE... AHENELZINE...
AMITRIPTYLINE... BENZEDRINE... DIAZEPAM...
MEPROBAMATE...

TAKES OUT ONE PILL FROM EACH THE TEMAZEPAM AND
MEPROBAMATE BOTTLES.

INT. MOM'S BEDROOM, APARTMENT—NIGHT

Arthur sets the food down in front of his mother lying in bed.
The TV's on, playing the local news.

PENNY

He must not be getting my
letters.

Arthur sits down on a small chair in front of an old vanity,
table covered with his mother's makeup.

ARTHUR

It's Thomas Wayne, Mom. He's a
busy man.

PENNY

Please. I worked for that family
for years. He always had a smile
for me. Least he could do is write
back.

ARTHUR

Ma, eat. You need to eat.

PENNY

You need to eat. Look how
skinny you are.

Before Arthur can say anything, his mother points to the
news on the TV—

PENNY

All day long it's more bad news.

That's all there is.

ARTHUR

Maybe you shouldn't watch so
much television.

PENNY

Thomas Wayne is our only
hope. He'll make a great mayor.
Everybody says so.

ARTHUR
(playful)
Everybody who? Who do you
talk to?

PENNY

Well everybody on the news.

(beat)
He's the only one who can save
this city. He owes it to us.

Arthur smiles for his mother as he cuts up some more of
her food.

PENNY
(she pats the bed)
Come sit. It's starting.

Arthur gets into bed with her, their nightly ritual. Stay on his
face as he watches the opening to their favorite show—

> BARRY O'DONNELL (OS ON TV)
> *From NCB Studios in Gotham*
> *City, it's "Live with Murray*
> *Franklin!" Tonight, Murray*
> *welcomes, Sandra Winger,*
> *comedian Skip Byron and the*
> *piano stylings of Yeldon &*
> *Chantel!*

ANGLE ON TELEVISION, intro to "LIVE WITH MURRAY
FRANKLIN!" playing—

> BARRY O'DONNELL (ON TV)
> *Joining Murray as always, Ellis*
> *Drane and his Jazz Orchestra.*
> *And me, I'm "that guy" Barry*
> *O'Donnell. And now, without*
> *further ado—Murraaaaay*
> *Franklin!*

INT. TALK SHOW SET, STAGE—STUDIO 4B—CONTINUOUS

SPOTLIGHT ON SHIMMERING MULTICOLORED CURTAINS
PARTING, AND OUT DANCES MURRAY FRANKLIN (late
60s) doing an old soft shoe to the jazzy tune Ellis Drane is
playing him out to. Audience cheering and applauding loudly
for him. Murray takes a little bow, and does one or two more
steps to the music...

ANGLE ON ARTHUR, clapping in the middle of the crowd.
He's dressed "richer" (it's Arthur's fantasy version of
himself). Everybody around him is enthusiastically
applauding Murray.

MURRAY FRANKLIN
(looking into the crowd)
Thank you. Glad you're here.
We've got a great looking
audience tonight.

Murray motions for everybody to quiet down, nodding his
head in appreciation of their applause—

MURRAY FRANKLIN
Wow. Thank you.

He glances up at Arthur, who is clapping wildly, squints his
eyes a bit to make him out—

MURRAY FRANKLIN
Thank you.

(beat; smiling)
Who's that there? Hey Bobby,
can you raise the lights for me?

The house lights come up. Murray takes a few steps
downstage and points straight up at Arthur—

MURRAY FRANKLIN
You there, will you stand up?
What's your name?

Arthur looks around at the people around him, and
realizes Murray's talking to him. Murray picked him out
of the crowd—Arthur gets up to his feet. He talks more
here, and with more confidence, looks more at ease than
we've seen him.

Hi Murray. Arthur. My name is
Arthur.

MURRAY FRANKLIN
There's something special about
you Arthur, I can tell. Where
you from?

ARTHUR
I live right here in the city. With
my mother. The audience starts
to giggle and laugh at him.

Murray holds up his hand, stopping them from laughing,
coming to Arthur's defense—

MURRAY FRANKLIN
Hold on. There's nothing funny
about that. I lived with my
mother before I made it. It was
just me and her. I'm that kid
whose father went out for a
pack of cigarettes and never
came back.

Audience "awwwws" for Murray, we can hear how much
empathy they have for him.

Arthur looks around at the crowd surrounding him.

ARTHUR
I know what that's like, Murray.
I've been the man of the house

for as long as I can remember.
I take good care of my mother.

The audience starts to applaud Arthur.

>   MURRAY FRANKLIN
> All that sacrifice. She must love
> you very much.

>   ARTHUR
> She does. She always tells me to
> smile and put on a happy face.
> She says that I was put here to
> spread joy and laughter.

>   MURRAY FRANKLIN
> What? Hold on. Can you say that
> again?

>   ARTHUR
>   (beaming with pride)
> My mother told me I had a
> purpose, to bring laughter and
> joy to the world.

Murray Franklin nods in approval, and claps his hands
loudly along with the rest of his audience, cheering for
Arthur—

>   MURRAY FRANKLIN
> Wow. I like that. I like that a lot.

INT. MOM'S BEDROOM, APARTMENT—CONTINUOUS

Arthur looks over at his mother lying next to him, her eyes glued to the TV, hears the studio audience applauding, blue light flickering over her face—

CUT TO:

ANGLE ON ARTHUR, listening to the audience applauding him, their applause getting louder and louder. He makes himself smile as wide as he can to show them he's happy.

Sees Murray Franklin waving for him to come down out of the crowd... First Arthur shakes his head no thanks... Sees BARRY O'DONNELL (60s), Murray's announcer, also waving him down... And Arthur finally relents and makes his way to the stage... joining Murray under the lights.

MURRAY TAKES ARTHUR'S HAND, RAISES IT ABOVE THEIR HEADS AND LEADS HIM IN TAKING A DEEP BOW... The audience goes crazy. Murray leans in and whispers something to Arthur, who laughs.

> MURRAY FRANKLIN
> (turns, looks into TV camera)
> Okay, we got a big show tonight,
> stay tuned. We'll be right back.

Ellis Drane and his Jazz Orchestra plays them to the commercial break... house lights go back down... cameras start moving to their next position... Murray puts an arm around Arthur, a private moment between them.

> MURRAY FRANKLIN
> That was great, Arthur, thanks.
> I loved hearing what you had to
> say. Made my day.

ARTHUR

Thanks, Murray. You know I
grew up without a dad too. He
left right after I was born. I don't
know what I ever did to him,—

INT. TALK SHOW SET, STAGE—STUDIO 4B—CONTINUOUS

Murray pulls Arthur in closer, lowers his voice—

MURRAY FRANKLIN

Fuck him. Guy like that doesn't
deserve you, Arthur. You see all
this, the lights, the show, the, the
love of the audience, I'd give it
all up in a heartbeat to have a
son like you.

Arthur looks at Murray Franklin, tears in his eyes and
Murray looks back at him and gives him a hug.

INT. HA-HA'S TALENT BOOKING, LOCKER ROOM—DAY

The cramped locker room of a small talent booking agency.
This is where Arthur works. They "rent out" talent for
parties and events. Clowns, magicians, male strippers.

Arthur takes off his shirt in front of his open locker,
grimacing in pain as he moves. His body's bruised from
the beating he took chasing after his sign.

RANDALL (OS)

You okay?

He turns. A fellow party clown, RANDALL (mid 50s), big bear
of a know-it-all, is opening his own locker putting his dry-
cleaned clown suit inside.

RANDALL
I heard about the beat down you
took. Fucking savages.

ARTHUR
It was just a bunch of kids. I
should have left it alone.

Randall searches through his messy locker, going through all
the bags inside—

RANDALL
No, they'll take everything from
you if you do that, all the crazy
shit out there, they're animals,—

ARTHUR (nods)
My mother says that people
nowadays lack empathy.

RANDALL
What's empathy?

ARTHUR
It means like "feeling for other
people."

RANDALL
Like sympathy?

ARTHUR
Kind of. But different.

Randall comes over, hands Arthur a brown paper bag—
Arthur looks inside, sees a GUN, a .38 SNUB-NOSED
REVOLVER.

Arthur looks back up at Randall, confused—

> RANDALL
> Take it. You gotta protect
> yourself out there. Or you're
> gonna get fucked.

As Arthur stares at the gun—

> ARTHUR
> (whispering)
> Randall, I'm not supposed to
> have a gun.

> RANDALL
> Don't sweat it, Art. No one has to
> know. And you can pay me back
> some other time. You know
> you're my boy.

That lands with Arthur, he smiles to himself. Stuffs the brown
paper bag into his locker and continues getting dressed.

Randall leans over and nudges Arthur, motioning to another
clown, GARY (30s), a dwarf, coming into the locker room
from their boss's office—

> GARY
> Arthur,—Hoyt wants to see you
> in his office.Before Arthur can
> ask why, Randall interrupts
> him—

> RANDALL
> Hey Gary, you know what I've
> always wondered?

GARY
(he knows what's coming)
What?

RANDALL
Do you people call it miniature
golf or is it just golf to you?

Randall cracks up at his own dumb joke—Gary just stares at him, this is apparently their thing. Arthur's not sure if he should laugh or not—

INT. FRONT OFFICE, HA-HA'S TALENT BOOKING—DAY

Arthur still half-dressed, walks into the cramped office.

His boss, HOYT VAUGHN (60s) sits behind a metal desk. The office is a complete mess, newspapers and files litter the desk. A giant ashtray filled with cigarette butts. A calendar of booking hangs on the wall. A scribbled, jumbled mess.

ARTHUR
Hey Hoyt. Gary said you wanted
to see me?

HOYT
(without even looking up)
How's the comedy career? Are
you a famous stand-up yet?

ARTHUR
Not quite. Haven't even
performed yet. Just been
working my material. This
business is all about fine-tuning.

Now Hoyt looks up. Takes a drag from his cigarette.

> HOYT
>
> Right.

Arthur goes to sit down—

> HOYT
>
> Don't sit. This will be quick.

Arthur stops in his tracks.

> HOYT
>
> Look, I like you, Arthur. A lot of
> the guys here, they think you're
> a freak. But I like you. I don't
> even know why I like you. I
> mean, you don't say much.
>
> (beat)
> It's probably that stupid laugh.
> It gets me every time. Kills me.

Unsure how to respond, Arthur just nods.

> HOYT
>
> But I got another complaint.
> And it's starting to piss me off.

Arthur takes a deep breath, and just smiles.

> HOYT
>
> Kenny's Music. The guy said you
> disappeared. Never even
> returned his sign.

ARTHUR
No. I got jumped. Didn't you
hear?

HOYT
For a sign? Bullshit. It makes no
sense, just give him his sign
back. He's going out of business
for god's—

ARTHUR
(interrupting)
Why would I keep his sign?

HOYT
(snaps)
How the fuck do I know, why
does anybody do anything?
Listen, if you don't return the
sign I gotta take it outta your
paycheck, you clear?

ARTHUR JUST LOOKS BACK AT HOYT AND KEEPS
SMILING, like it hurts his face.

CUT TO:

EXT. BACK ALLEY, OUTSIDE HA-HA'S—DAY

WE'RE AT THE FAR END OF AN ALLEY, about halfway down,
catch a glimpse of Arthur still half-dressed on the other side of a
dumpster. From this vantage, all we can see is him furiously
KICKING and STOMPING on something... or somebody.

We don't hear anything. And we can't make out what it is that
he's so violently beating down.

It could be a cat... a cardboard box... a homeless person...
We don't know.

Arthur just continues unleashing his rage—

INT. CITY BUS (MOVING)—HEADING UPTOWN—LATE DAY

Arthur at the end of his work day, sitting in his spot toward
the back of the bus.

Across the aisle from him, he's innocently watching a young
couple, playfully teasing each other.

EXT. STREETS, THE BRONX—SUNSET

Arthur heading back home down the litter-covered streets
like he does every night. Garbage still piled along the sidewalks, some burning in trash cans, air still thick with smog.

He's carrying the paper bag that Randall gave him.

EXT. SIDE ALLEY, TENEMENTS—EARLY DUSK

Arthur cuts through the alley, a couple of the young kids are
smoking on the fire escape.

EXT. STEEP STAIRWAY, TENEMENTS—DUSK

Arthur trudging up the endless staircase, step-after-step-
after-step-after—

INT. LOBBY, APARTMENT BUILDING—DUSK

Arthur checks his mailbox. Empty.

INT. ELEVATOR, APARTMENT BUILDING—DUSK

Arthur is on the elevator, as the door closes, he hears—

SOPHIE (OS)
Wait!!

He puts his foot out with some panache to stop the closing door—He's a romantic at heart. *Ding.*

And SOPHIE (late 20s), African-American, looking harried, tired eyes, steps onto the elevator with her 5-YEAR-OLD DAUGHTER who's holding onto a doll, talking to her mother about what she wants for her birthday.

Arthur moves to the back of the elevator—

Sophie nods thanks. The doors wheeze shut, pausing for a moment before they close—

Arthur holds his breath, hoping he doesn't start to laugh. Elevator rises, halting at first. Floors dinging.

Suddenly the elevator shudders hard, making a loud groaning sound. Flickering lights cut off, then come back on.

SOPHIE
(shaking her head; to Arthur)
This building is just so awful,
isn't it?

Arthur nods yes... he doesn't know what to say. The little girl just keeps babbling about what she wants for her birthday.

Sophie can't take it any more, looks over at Arthur and mimes blowing her head off with her finger—

Arthur's eyes go wide.

The doors open. They all step off.

Sophie grabs her daughter's hand and walks down the hall in the opposite direction of Arthur.

He just stands there for a beat. Heart beating fast.

> ARTHUR
> (calls out after her)
> Hey—

She turns around.

And Arthur mimes blowing his head off with *his* finger— Sophie doesn't know what to say, just forces a strained smile back at him.

INT. MOM'S APARTMENT, BATHROOM—NIGHT

ARTHUR'S GIVING HIS MOM A BATH, being careful with her as he shampoos her hair.

He fills an empty plastic container with some bath water.

> ARTHUR
> Look up.

> PENNY
> Maybe the mailman's throwing
> them away.

She tilts her head back and he rinses her hair with the water from the container...

ARTHUR

Mom, why are these letters so
important to you? What do you
think he's gonna do?

PENNY

He's gonna help us.

ARTHUR

Help us how?

PENNY

Get us out of here, take me away
from this place and these—these
people.

ARTHUR

You worked for him over 30
years ago. What makes you
think he would help us?

Penny looks at him with conviction, water dripping down her
face, into her eyes. She wipes it away with her hands—

PENNY

Because Thomas Wayne is a
good man. If he knew how I was
living, if he saw this place, it
would make him sick. I can't
explain it to you any better
than that.

Arthur nods. Annoyed, but not worth the argument.

ARTHUR

I don't want you worrying
about money. Everyone's been
telling me they think my stand-
up is ready for the big clubs. It's
just a matter of time before I get
a break.

PENNY

Happy, what makes you think
you could do that?

ARTHUR

What do you mean?

PENNY

I mean, don't you have to be
funny to be a comedian?

Beat.

INT. MOM'S BEDROOM, APARTMENT—LATE NIGHT

Penny is out cold in her bedroom, a half-eaten plate of food is
next to her on the bed.

INT. LIVING ROOM, MOM'S APARTMENT—CONTINUOUS

Arthur sits on the couch. The 1937 version of "Shall We
Dance" is playing on the TV. He holds the .38 SNUB-NOSED
REVOLVER Randall gave him in his hand. He's never held a
gun before, looks uncomfortable with it, the weight of it in
his hand...

He stares at it for a moment, then points it at the black-and-white movie playing on TV, hand trembling a bit... Points it at the chair his mother sits on... Points it at his head.

BLAMMMMMMM!

He jumps up off the couch. What the fuck!? He looks around in a panic. His hands shaking.

He shot a hole in the wall.

> PENNY (OS)
> (awoken by the shot)
> HAPPY!? What was that? Are
> you okay?

> ARTHUR
> What?!

He quickly turns up the TV volume, A GROUP OF MEN WORKING ON A SHIP SINGING "SLAP THAT BASS" TO FRED ASTAIRE—

> PENNY (OS)
> THAT NOISE! DID YOU HEAR
> THAT NOISE?

ASTAIRE NOW SINGING AND DANCING FOR THE OTHER MEN, Arthur shouts back to his mother as he shoves the gun under the couch cushions—

> ARTHUR
> I'M WATCHING AN OLD WAR
> MOVIE.

> PENNY (OS)
> TURN IT DOWN!

He heads for his mother's bedroom.

INT. MOM'S BEDROOM, DOORWAY—CONTINUOUS

Arthur looks in on his mom in her dark bedroom, can make out the outline of her body sitting up.

> PENNY
> It's so loud.

> ARTHUR
> I know. The Americans are
> really giving it to the Japs.

He walks over to Penny in the darkness. Kisses her on the forehead.

> ARTHUR
> (softly)
> I'm sorry. I'll turn it down.

INT. KITCHEN, MOM'S APARTMENT—LATE NIGHT

Arthur is writing in his journal. He speaks softly to himself as he writes...

> ARTHUR
> Why didn't Randall tell me the
> gun was loaded? I could have
> killed someone.
>
> (beat)
> I could have killed myself.

CLOSE ON THE LAST LINE, he crosses out "could"... Writes... "should"

ARTHUR
(still to himself)
I should have killed myself.

CLOSE ON ARTHUR as he crosses out something again...

ARTHUR
(louder to himself)
I should kill myself.

Beat.

EXT. STEEP STAIRWAY, TENEMENTS—MORNING

SOPHIE AND GIGI MAKING THEIR WAY down the steep stairs, on their way to school. Sophie is dressed more conservatively than when we've previously seen her.

REVEAL, Arthur watching them from the top of the stairway, keeping his distance. He starts after them—

EXT. PUBLIC SCHOOL—MORNING

Sophie drops GiGi off at school. Arthur's watching them from a distance.

EXT. ELEVATED SUBWAY PLATFORM—MORNING

Sophie waits on the platform. Lights a cigarette.

We see Arthur, hidden behind a steel support beam— watching her from a distance.

EXT. STREET, FINANCIAL DISTRICT—MORNING

Towering buildings crowd the sky. White collar, white businessmen in suits. Still lots of trash, but it's piled high, neatly in black bags along the sidewalk.

Arthur's hanging across the street from Gotham First National Bank as Sophie enters the building. He's just standing there watching, trying to get the nerve to go inside.

Beat.

INT. GOTHAM COMEDY CLUB, CHINATOWN—NIGHT

Arthur sitting in the middle of a dark, crowded comedy club. People on dates. Groups of friends. All here to watch the stand-up. He sits at a small table by himself, watching the act on stage.

The comic on stage is killing it. The whole room is laughing and applauding. Everyone except Arthur. He's watching. Studying. Diligently jotting down notes in his notebook.

EXT. GOTHAM COMEDY CLUB, STREET—CHINATOWN—NIGHT

People are piling out of the club, onto the narrow street, jumble of lit-up signs, most glowing yellow or red. Arthur walks out alone, carrying his notebook. He sees a FLYER taped to the entrance of the club.

CLOSE ON THE FLYER, "Open mic night. Thursdays. 7pm." He rips the flyer off the wall.

INT. KITCHEN, MOM'S APARTMENT—LATE NIGHT

Arthur is writing in his journal. His mom is dead asleep. He opens his worn notebook. Flips to a page titled "Jokes" and starts writing—

CLOSE ON WORDS, as he slowly writes: "The worst part about having a mental illness is..."

ANGLE ON ARTHUR, pausing, thinking it over for a moment.

Then he laughs to himself when he comes up with something.

CLOSE ON WORDS, coming faster now, "...that people expect you to behave as if you don't."

He hears knocking on the front door—

INT. FRONT DOOR, MOM'S APARTMENT—CONTINUOUS

Arthur opening the door—

Sees Sophie standing there with attitude, leaning up against the door frame.

> SOPHIE
> Were you following me today?

> ARTHUR
> Yeah.

> SOPHIE
> I thought that was you. I was
> hoping you'd come in and rob
> the place.

Beat.

> ARTHUR
> (leans in, quietly)
> I have a gun. I could come by
> tomorrow.

> SOPHIE
> (laughing)
> You're so funny, Arthur.

ARTHUR

You know, I do stand-up
comedy. You should maybe
come see a show sometime.

SOPHIE

I could do that.

ARTHUR

Yeah?

SOPHIE

You'll let me know when?

ARTHUR

Yeah.

And she just turns and walks away toward her apartment—

INT. HA-HA'S TALENT BOOKING, LOCKER ROOM—DAY

Arthur is putting on his makeup, using the small mirror in
his locker. Behind him a couple other clowns are eating their
lunch at a small table, not paying Arthur any attention.

Arthur pauses half-finished, and stares at himself for a beat.
Hooks the corners of his mouth down with his index fingers,
turning his mouth into the "tragedy mask" frown—

And then he pulls his fingers up, pulling them up wider and
wider, stretching his smile into a grotesque parody of the
"comedy mask," trying to make himself look happy, pulling
his mouth so wide tears come to his eyes—

PRE-LAP SCRATCHY OLD-TIME FOLK RECORDING OF "If
You're Happy and You Know It"—

"OLD-TIME" VOICE (RECORD)
(singing, strumming guitar)
—*if you're happy and you know it
and you really want to show it, if
you're happy and you know it
clap your hands.*

INT. GOTHAM GENERAL HOSPITAL—CHILDREN'S WARD—LATE DAY

Arthur lip-syncing and strumming an air guitar along to the song (like a Dennis Potter musical), for a ward full of sick children. He's wearing an oversized white lab coat over his clown costume. A few nurses and doctors watch as well, song blaring from a small record player—

                    ARTHUR
                  (lip-syncing)
              If you're happy and you know it,
              stomp your feet.

Arthur stomps his feet to the song... All the kids stomping
along with the recording...

                    ARTHUR
                  (lip-syncing)
              If you're happy and you know it,
              stomp your feet.

                  (stomp, stomp)
              If you're happy and you know it
              and you really want to show it, if
              you're happy and you know it
              stomp your feet.

And Arthur stomps harder, trying to make the kids laugh
and—

HIS .38 SNUB-NOSED REVOLVER slips out from the bottom
of his pants, sliding across the floor—

ARTHUR STOPS SINGING, EVERYBODY LOOKS AT THE
GUN as it clatters to a stop on the floor. "If You're Happy and
You Know It" still playing on the record player...

EXT. PHONE BOOTH, GOTHAM GENERAL HOSPITAL—DUSK

Arthur's in a cramped graffiti-covered phone booth on a busy
street corner outside Gotham General, trash piled high. He's
in his street clothes, clown-face still painted on, green wig
still on his head.

ARTHUR (into phone)
Hoyt, let me explain.

HOYT (OVER PHONE)
Oh, this'll be good. Please tell me
why you brought a gun into a
kid's hospital?

ARTHUR (into phone)
It was, it was a prop gun. It's
part of my act now.

HOYT (OVER PHONE)
Bullshit. What kinda clown
carries a fucking gun? Besides,
Randall told me you tried to buy
a .38 off him last week.

Arthur's taken aback that Randall would do that to him.

ARTHUR
(into phone)
Randall told you that?

HOYT (OVER PHONE)
He was with me when the call
came in. You're a fuck up,
Arthur. And a liar. You're fired.

ARTHUR
(into phone)
Hoyt, please I love this job—

HOYT (OVER PHONE)
Say it, Arthur.

(beat)
Let me hear you say it.

ARTHUR
(into phone)
Say what?

HOYT (OVER PHONE)
I'm a fuck up and I'm fired.

ARTHUR
(into phone; low)
—I'm a fuck up and I'm fired.

HOYT (OVER PHONE)
Louder.

ARTHUR
(into phone; louder)
I'm a fuck up and I'm fired.

The line goes dead.

INT. SUBWAY (MOVING)—NIGHT

ARTHUR SITTING ON THE SUBWAY CONTEMPLATING
WHAT JUST WENT DOWN, face still painted, his clown gear
in a shopping bag on the seat next to him, green wig on his lap.

Subway car near empty. Arthur's sitting across from a lonely-
looking MIDDLE-AGED WOMAN, there's also a YOUNG
WOMAN (late 20s) reading a book at the far end.

Arthur glances at the Middle-Aged Woman, maybe trying to
make a connection, but the woman doesn't even notice him as
the train comes to a stop, her head's somewhere else—

The woman gets off the train, and THREE WALL STREET
GUYS get on. They're loud and obnoxious, clearly drunk.
One of them is eating some french fries out of a greasy
McDonald's bag.

He flops down on the bench across from the young woman,
and checks her out. The other two guys start getting into it
with each other—

> WALL STREET #1
> —I'm telling you, she wanted my
> number. We should have just
> stayed. The train starts moving
> again...

> WALL STREET #2
> You're dreaming, man. She
> wasn't interested—at all.

> WALL STREET #1
> Are you nuts? Did you see how
> close we were dancing!? She was
> in love, bro.

He starts dancing a bit with himself, mimicking what he
remembers. Wall Street #2 takes a swig from the brown bag
he is carrying.

> WALL STREET #2
> She couldn't wait to get away
> from you.

Arthur's watching them closely, impressed by their
confidence and easy-going camaraderie.

WALL STREET #1
(to the third guy)
Ryan, am I crazy? Tell him what
you saw.

But the third Wall Street guy isn't paying his friends any
attention. He has his eyes set on the young woman sitting
across from him, reading her book.

WALL STREET #3
(to the girl)
Hey. You want some french
fries?

He holds out his McDonald's bag and shakes it to get her
attention. The other two share a look. Arthur watches from
his seat.

WALL STREET #3
Hello? I'm talking to you. You
want some fries?

She looks up and shakes her head, polite smile.

YOUNG WOMAN
No thank you.

The other two guys crack up at this apparent blow-off. The
third Wall Street guy shakes his head, embarrassed, and
starts softly flinging fries at the young woman.

WALL STREET #3
You sure? They're really good.

She just buries her face deeper in her book—

Don't ignore him. He's being
nice to you.

One of the french fries lands in her hair. She looks down
toward Arthur, looking to see if he's going to do something or
say something—

Arthur just sits there nervous. Not sure what to do, or even if
he wants to do anything at all.

AND HE JUST BURSTS OUT LAUGHING. He covers his mouth
with his wig as they continue to harass the woman.

They all look over—What the fuck is this clown laughing at?

WALL STREET #1
Something funny, asshole?

With their attention diverted, the young woman rushes out
through the door between subway cars, glancing back at
Arthur before she goes—

WALL STREET #3
(shouts after her)
BITCH!

He laughs even harder through his green wig. The Wall
Street guys turn to him sitting by himself at the end of
the car—

Arthur sees them staring. Looks down at the ground, hand
still covering his mouth, face turning red. Subway swaying,
lights flickering on and off.

Beat.

One of the guys heads down the car toward Arthur, starts singing "Send in the Clowns" as he approaches—

> WALL STREET #1
> (singing)
> *Isn't it rich?*

> (MORE)
> WALL STREET #1 (CONT'D)
> *Are we a pair?*
> *Me here, at last on the ground*
> *You in midair.*
> *Send in the clowns.*

The others crack up and follow after him. The guy plops down next to Arthur, puts his arm around his shoulder as he sings—

> ARTHUR
> (shakes his head, stifling the laughter)
> Please. Don't.

> WALL STREET #1
> (continues singing to him)
> *Isn't it bliss?*
> *Don't you approve?*
> *One who keeps tearing around,*
> *One who can't move.*

Arthur starts to get up—The lead guy pulls him back down.

> WALL STREET #1
> *Where are the clowns?*
> *There ought to be clowns.*

As he finishes the song, Arthur's laughing fit is coming to an end. One of the other guys sits down on the other side of him. He's now sandwiched in between them—

> WALL STREET #2
> So tell us, buddy. What's so
> fucking funny?

> ARTHUR
> Nothing. I have a condition—

Arthur reaches into his shopping bag to get one of his "Forgive my laughter" cards, the third guy sees him reaching and tries to grab the bag from him—

Arthur pulls on it—

> ARTHUR
> No. It's just my stuff. I don't have
> anything.The guy rips the bag
> from his hand—

> WALL STREET #3
> I'll tell you what you have,
> asshole.

Arthur gets up from between them to go grab his bag back. The two guys are cracking up.

> WALL STREET #3
> You want it back? Here—

Arthur reaches out to grab the bag—

And the guy tosses it over his head to one of his friends. Keeping it away from Arthur.

Three guys in suits tossing a shopping bag around, playing 'monkey in the middle' with a clown AND WE HEAR the drum roll opening to BOBBY SHORT singing "Send in the Clowns" Live at the Café Carlyle.

Arthur keeps trying to catch his bag until suddenly—

WHAP! Out of nowhere one of the guys punches him hard in the face.

Arthur goes down as if in slow motion. Blood coming from his nose. He tries to get up, but his feet slip from under him and he falls back down—

> WALL STREET #1
> Stay down you freak.

And the third Wall Street guy starts kicking him—

The others join in. Surrounding Arthur on the ground, kicking him deliberately, sadistically, and the music swells—

BLAM!

Wall Street #1 falls back dead. Blood splattering on the subway wall behind him—

And we HEAR Bobby Short sing out, picking up from where the Wall Street Guy left off—

> BOBBY SHORT (SINGING)
> *Just when I'd stopped*
> *opening doors*
> *Finally knowin' the one that I*
> *wanted was yours*

BLAM! BLAM! Wall Street #2 goes down—

Revealing Arthur on the ground, opening his eyes to see what he did, blood dripping from his nose, smoking gun in hand—

> **BOBBY SHORT (SINGING)**
> *Making my entrance again with*
> *my usual flair*
> *Sure of my lines*
> *No one is there*

The third guy takes off running for the doors that separate the cars.

Arthur starts after him, but then stops... turns back to grab his bag and his wig, his hands shaking from the adrenaline.

The train is coming to a stop.

> **BOBBY SHORT (SINGING)**
> *Don't you love farce?*
> *My fault I fear . . .*

Arthur grabs the green wig from between the two dead bodies, blood everywhere, and stuffs it into his shopping bag—

The subway doors wheeze open and Arthur steps halfway off the train, waiting to see if the third Wall Street guy gets off in the car ahead of him. Arthur sees him run off—

EXT. SUBWAY PLATFORM—CONTINUOUS

The platform is empty, the Wall Street guy is running toward the stairs—

Arthur follows, blood still dripping from his nose—Behind them, the train pulls away—

> BOBBY SHORT (SINGING)
> *I thought that you'd want what I want.*
> *Sorry, my dear.*

The guy makes his way to the stairs, unaware that Arthur is behind him—

BLAM!

The third guy falls, tumbling down the stairs. Arthur walks over to the body and empties the chamber—BLAM! BLAM!

> BOBBY SHORT (SINGING)
> *But where are the clowns?*
> *Quick, send in the clowns*
> *Don't bother they're here.*

BLAM! He's got nothing left.

EXT. ROBINSON PARK SUBWAY STATION—NIGHT

Arthur hauls ass up the stairs, rushing out of the station, the song still playing—

EXT. STREET, ROBINSON PARK—NIGHT

Bounding past bags of garbage, he leaps over a pile, taking a turn into a run-down needle park, the lights of garbage fires flickering in the darkness.

INT. PUBLIC BATHROOM, ROBINSON PARK—NIGHT

Arthur bursts into the small bathroom, out of breath. Overwhelmed, vibrating with emotions. He leans his forehead against the door, sweat dripping down his face, and catches his breath.

Arthur feels all those emotions running through his body, can feel them all. He sticks his right foot out and starts to slowly turn, his right arm rising slowly above his head as his right foot leads, turning like something is awakening inside of him—

Sweat dripping down his face, "Send in the Clowns" finally comes to an end. He starts washing the blood and clown makeup off his sweaty face.

Looks up at his smudged reflection in the dirty mirror, water dripping, white grease paint running off his face—

Beat.

INT. APARTMENT BUILDING, HALLWAY—NIGHT

ARTHUR FLOATING OUT OF THE ELEVATOR AND DOWN THE HALLWAY AS IF IN A DREAM, coming up on Sophie's door and knocking—

She opens the door and sees Arthur standing there—

And before Sophie can say anything Arthur leans and kisses her and—

Sophie kisses him back and pulls him inside her apartment, closing the door behind them—

CUT TO:

INT. HA-HA'S TALENT BOOKING, LOCKER ROOM—MORNING

Arthur walks into the locker room, sees Randall half-dressed for work, sitting with Gary, TWO OTHER CLOWNS AND A HANDSOME "CHIPPENDALES" DANCER around the small table, shooting the shit, drinking coffee.

They nod hello at Arthur or give him a perfunctory wave, most of his co-workers think he's a freak.

> GARY
> Hey Art, I heard what
> happened—
>
> I'm sorry man.

> RANDALL
> Yeah, Hoyt did you wrong,
> buddy.
>
> Doesn't seem fair.

Arthur looks hard at Randall for a moment, just slowly nods, and continues on to his locker.

He starts to clean it out, stuffing all of his clown gear into an old brown paper shopping bag. Hears them talking about him behind his back, about why he got fired, laughing at him—

                    HA-HA CLOWN #1 (OS)
              Did you really bring a gun to the
              kid's hospital, Artie? What the
              fuck would you do that for?

Arthur doesn't answer them, just continues emptying his
locker, a bag of balloons, a magic wand, some trick flowers—

                    CHIPPENDALES
              No, I heard he pulled it out and
              waved it around like a cowboy.

His coworkers crack up. Arthur answers the guy without
looking back—

                    ARTHUR
              It was a prop gun. And I didn't
              pull it out, it fell out.

                    CHIPPENDALES
              So is that part of your new act? If
              your dancing doesn't do the
              trick, you just gonna shoot
              yourself?

More laughter.

                    HA-HA CLOWN #2
              I thought your clown was a
              lover, Artie, not a fighter,—

Arthur turns and looks at all of them, nods at Randall—

                    ARTHUR
              Why don't you ask Randall
              about it? It was his gun.

> RANDALL
> What? Stop talking outta your
> ass, Art! (to the guys)
>
> I think all his stupid laughing
> musta scrambled his brain or
> something.

The guys laugh and keep jawing. Arthur doesn't say anything. Just finishes packing up his bag and closes his locker door—

INT. STAIRWAY, HA-HA'S TALENT BOOKING—MORNING

> Arthur walks down the stairs,
> brown shopping bag under
> his arm.
>
> Behind him, Randall follows him
> into the stairway—

> RANDALL
> Hey, Art, hold up,—

Arthur stops, turns around.

> RANDALL
> What the hell was that about?
> Why would you say that?

> ARTHUR
> What?

> RANDALL
> (lowers his voice)
> That it was *my idea* about the

gun. That subway shit's no joke, you know, they got sketches of clowns on the front of every newspaper,—

ARTHUR
I don't know what you're talking about, Randall.

RANDALL
(looks at him)
Right. Okay. I just want to make sure you got your head on straight.

Arthur just looks back at him and smiles.

ARTHUR
My heads right here.

Randall nods, maybe it's sinking in with Arthur.

RANDALL
Good. I don't even know if you did it but there's no need to draw any attention to yourself, y'know? Or we're both fucked.

ARTHUR
What are you worried about, Randall? You didn't kill three assholes on the subway, did you?

RANDALL
Of course I didn't.

                    ARTHUR
                   (continuing)
            You didn't shoot one point blank
            in the head. The other one twice
            in the chest, before chasing the
            third one down and shooting him
            three times in the back, right?

Arthur puts his fingers forming a gun to Randall's head,
stares straight at him—

                    ARTHUR
                    (singing)
            Isn't it rich? Are we a pair?

Then turns and heads down the stairs, keeps singing "Send in
the Clowns"—

                    ARTHUR
            Me here at last on the ground,
            You in midair.
            Send in the clowns.
            Where are the clowns?
            Don't bother, they're here.

                                              CUT TO:

INT. MOM'S APARTMENT, KITCHEN—MORNING

CLOSE ON A COUPLE OF PILLS BOTTLES, THEY'RE NEARLY
EMPTY NOW.

                    PENNY (OS)
            Happy, look Thomas Wayne is
            on TV.

                    ARTHUR
            Yes, mother.

Arthur swallows a few of the pills...

> PENNY (OS)
> They're interviewing him about
> those horrible murders on the
> subway.

He glances at the TV playing in the living room through the
open wall—

> ARTHUR
> Why are they talking to him?

INT. MOM'S LIVING ROOM, APARTMENT—CONTINUOUS

Penny shushes him, she's sitting in her chair, watching one of
those "Good Morning, Gotham" shows.

> PENNY
> He looks like he gained weight.

> THOMAS WAYNE (ON TV)
> All three of them worked at
> Wayne Investments. They were
> good, decent, educated.

A small smirk registers on Arthur's face when photos of the
THREE WALL STREET GUYS come up on the screen.

> THOMAS WAYNE (ON TV)
> And while I didn't know them
> personally, like all Wayne
> employees, they were family.

Arthur's mom sits up in her chair—

PENNY
You hear that! I told you. We're
family.

ANGLE ON TELEVISION, footage of GRAFFITI around the
city. "KILL THE RICH" spray painted on a storefront.

"F*CK WALL STREET" written on a subway wall. "RESIST"
scrawled across a billboard.

"GOOD MORNING" HOST (ON TV)
There now seems to be a
groundswell of anti-rich
sentiment in the city. It's almost
as if our less-fortunate residents
have taken the side of the killer.

THOMAS WAYNE (ON TV)
Yes and it's a shame. It's one of
the reasons I'm considering a
run for mayor. Gotham has lost
its way.

"GOOD MORNING" HOST (ON TV)
Are you announcing your
candidacy?

THOMAS WAYNE (ON TV)
(smiles)
No comment.

We hear Penny gasp, excited.

"GOOD MORNING" HOST (ON TV)
What about the eyewitness
report of the suspect being a

man in clown makeup or a
clown mask?

A smile starts to creep across Arthur's face—The camera
zooms in closer to Thomas Wayne on the screen—

> THOMAS WAYNE (ON TV)
> It makes total sense to me. What
> kind of coward would do
> something that cold-blooded?
> Someone who hides behind a
> mask. Someone who's envious of
> those more fortunate than
> themselves, yet too scared to
> show their own face.
>
> (to camera)
> And until those kind of people
> change for the better, those of us
> who've made a good life for
> ourselves will always look at
> those who haven't as nothing
> but clowns.

INT. DEPT. OF HEALTH, OFFICE—DAY

Arthur sits across from the same Social Worker from the
opening scene. Same depressing office. He takes a drag from
his cigarette—

> ARTHUR
> —I heard this song on the radio
> the other day. This guy was
> singing that his name was
> Carnival.

(sings)
*"Rise and fall, spin and call, and
my name is Carnival."*

SOCIAL WORKER
Arthur—

ARTHUR
Which is crazy because that's
my clown name at work. And
until a little while ago it was like
nobody ever saw me. Even I
didn't know if I really existed.

SOCIAL WORKER
Arthur, I have some bad news
for you.

ARTHUR
You don't listen, do you? I don't
think you ever really hear me.
You just ask the same questions
every week. *"How's your job?"*
*"Are you having any negative
thoughts?"*

(beat)
All I have are negative thoughts.
But you don't listen anyway. I
said, "for my whole life I didn't
know if I even really existed."
But I do. And people are starting
to notice—

> SOCIAL WORKER
> They've cut our funding. We're
> closing down our offices next
> week.

He looks around, just noticing some MOVING BOXES stacked
against the wall.

> SOCIAL WORKER
> The city's cut funding across the
> board. Social services is part of
> that. This is the last time we'll be
> meeting.

Arthur nods, not hating the idea.

> ARTHUR
> Okay.

> SOCIAL WORKER
> They don't give a shit about
> people like you, Arthur. And,
> they really don't really give a
> shit about people like me either.

Arthur sits there for a moment. And then it dawns on him—

> ARTHUR
> How am I supposed to get my
> medication now? Who do I talk
> to?

> SOCIAL WORKER
> I'm sorry, Arthur.

He just stares at her, taking it all in.

INT. COMEDY CLUB, BACKSTAGE HALLWAY—NIGHT

ARTHUR'S POV, slowly walking down the hall—as if in slow motion—toward a set of stairs leading up to the back of the stage, spotlight bleeding through the curtain, other wannabe comics looking at him as he passes—

CLOSE ON ARTHUR, he's changed his hair, it's slicked back some, not quite as smooth as the Wall Street Guys, sweat beading on his forehead—

He climbs up the stairs—always climbing uphill—and waits at the edge of the curtain, pulls his worn, joke notebook out of his back pocket. Glancing into the room he sees it's a pretty good crowd. Sees Sophie taking a seat in the back.

Wheeling back into the stairway, he catches his breath in the shadows—

He hears the EMCEE from the stage.

> EMCEE (OS)
> This next comic describes
> himself as a lifelong Gotham
> resident who from a young age
> was always told that "his
> purpose in life was to bring
> laughter and joy into this cold,
> dark world." Ummm. Okay.

He hears the crowd laugh.

> EMCEE (OS)
> Please help me welcome Arthur
> Fleck!There is a smattering of
> applause.

INT. STAGE, COMEDY CLUB—CONTINUOUS

ARTHUR STEPPING ON STAGE, out under the spotlight, lifts
the microphone in front of his mouth, the light so bright he
can't see faces in the dark audience, his hand trembling
holding onto his worn notebook—

He takes a deep breath, looks out at the dark crowd, and
opens his mouth.

AND STARTS TO LAUGH. His eyes go wide. God no, not now.
A terrified look comes to his face under the laughter. He just
keeps laughing. The crowd is just staring back at him.

Finally he composes himself—

> ARTHUR
> (trying to stop himself from laughing)
> —good evening, hello.
>
> (deep breath; trying to stop laughing)
> Good to be here.
>
> (keeps cracking up)
> I, I hated school as a kid. But my
> mother would always say,—
>
> (bad imitation of his mom, still laughing)
> "You should enjoy it. One day
> you'll have to work for a living."
>
> (laughs)

"No I won't, Ma. I'm gonna be a comedian!"

Arthur keeps cracking up. Hard to hear anything or anybody else. He goes through his notebook trying to find another joke—

> ARTHUR
> (reading verbatim)
> It's funny, I was thinking the
> other day,—Why are rich people
> so confused by the poor people?

        (silently counting to three)
      Because they don't make any
      sense!

CLOSE ON ARTHUR, looking out into the audience, sees
Sophie sitting in the back laughing—

The MUSIC SWELLS...

                              CUT TO:

EXT. COMEDY CLUB, CHINATOWN STREET—NIGHT

Arthur and Sophie walking out of the club after the show.

They walk past a newsstand—a wall of Chinese language newspapers mixed with local papers and tabloids, screaming headlines about the three Wall Street Guys gunned down on the train.

Arthur stops and stares at the headlines—

CLOSE ON HEADLINES, "Subway Vigilante"... "Yuppie Slaughter"

"Killer Clown On The Loose?"...

SOPHIE (OS)
(re: the headlines)
You believe that shit?

(beat)
I'll bet you five bucks those rich
assholes deserved it.

He turns to her.

> ARTHUR
> You think?

> SOPHIE
> Look at their faces. Those smug
> smiles. I've seen that look. Fuck
> them.

Sophie flicks her cigarette away and starts walking.

> SOPHIE
> The guy who did it is a hero.
> Three less pricks in Gotham
> City. Woo-hoo! Only a million
> more to go.

Arthur watches her walk for a beat. She looks great, even in
front of the mounds of garbage bags that line the sidewalk.

A CAB rolls past. In the backseat, someone wearing a CLOWN
MASK stares back at Arthur. Holding his look for a moment.

INT. DONUT SHOP, BOOTH—NIGHT

A run-down donut shop.

Through the window we see Arthur and Sophie sitting across
from each other in a molded plastic booth. Bathed in ugly
fluorescent light, a few other patrons scattered about.

We don't hear what they're saying, but they look happy—
and Sophie is laughing. Hard.

Arthur stares at her, this may be the best night of his
entire life.

INT. MOM'S APARTMENT, LIVING ROOM—NIGHT

Arthur opening the door to his mother's apartment, holding
a box of donuts in his hand, sees the flickering blue light of

the TV on in the living room, hears the end of "LIVE WITH
MURRAY FRANKLIN!" He locks the locks, drawing the
security chain high on the door.

TURNS TO CATCH A GLIMPSE OF HIS MOTHER PASSED
OUT in the living room.

Arthur sets the box of donuts down and puts his face
up against his mom's nose, to see if she's breathing or if
she's dead—

ON THE TELEVISION Murray does his signature sign off, the one he's been doing for years—

> **MURRAY FRANKLIN (ON TV)**
> (looking into camera)
> Good night! And always
> remember,—

That's life.

He gently shakes her awake. Sweeping her up out of the chair as he hears Ellis Drane and his Jazz Orchestra close the show with an upbeat instrumental version of Frank Sinatra's "That's Life"...

> **MOM**
> (half-asleep)
> Happy, I wrote a new letter.

> **ARTHUR**
> (grabs her hand)
> C'mon, Ma, dance with me a
> little.

Arthur pulls his mother in close and starts dancing with her to the music, the only light coming from the television...

> **MOM**
> For Thomas Wayne. It's
> important.

She looks at him and smiles, dances with him a little... "That's Life" still playing from TV...

> **MOM**
> You smell like cologne.

ARTHUR
Cause I just had a big date.

MOM (laughing)
I'm going to bed. Just don't
forget to mail it.

She breaks away and walks toward her bedroom.

Arthur can't help but smile to himself as he takes off his jacket and throws it on the chair. He continues to slow dance with himself for a moment—He notices the envelope on the table, addressed to Thomas Wayne.

He stares at it for a beat. Cranes his neck toward his mother's bedroom, listening if she's still awake. And then—

Quietly rips it open, starts to read the letter: CLOSE ON WORDS, "Dearest Thomas, I don't know where else to turn..."

"We need your help..."

"Your son and I need help"

Stops reading, stays on—

"Your son"

He glances up at his mother's room, then back down at the words, "Your son"

ARTHUR STANDING IN THE MIDDLE OF THE LIVING ROOM staring at those two words like he's too afraid to move, lit up by the flickering blue light—

INT. MOM'S BEDROOM, APARTMENT—EARLY MORNING

ARTHUR'S SITTING IN A CHAIR in his mother's room watching her sleep. He has clearly been up all night. Still wearing the same clothes.

He's holding her letter in his hand as the sun is just starting to rise outside the windows, light just beginning to crack the gloom.

Arthur impatiently sits there for another moment waiting for his mother to wake up, then suddenly—

SHRIEKS OUT AT THE TOP OF HIS LUNGS like a teapot, kicking his back on the chair like an excited toddler—

Penny wakes with a start, looking around half asleep and confused—

> PENNY
> —what, what time is it?

He doesn't answer.

> PENNY
> What happened? Did you hurt
> yourself again?

Arthur holds her letter up in his hand.

> ARTHUR
> What is this? How come you
> never told me?

PENNY

Is, is that my letter? Is that <u>my</u>
personal letter, Happy?

(angry)
You have no right opening my
mail. Who do you think you
are?!

ARTHUR
(raising his voice; excited)
Apparently I'm Thomas
Wayne's son! How could you
keep that from me?

Penny slowly getting up out of bed.

PENNY
Stop yelling at me, you're gonna
kill me, give me a heart attack!
She goes into the bathroom.

ARTHUR (shouts after her)
I'm not yelling! I'm just, excited.
How can any of this be real!?

PENNY (OS)
(shouts back from behind the door)
I'm not talking to you until you
calm down.

Arthur paces for a minute, now goes to the bathroom door.
Talks to his mother from the behind the closed door.

ARTHUR
(lowers his voice; trying to sound calm)
Okay. How's this, Mom? Better?
Will you please talk to me?

Arthur leans in closer to the door. Leaning against it with just his head—

ARTHUR
Please.

PENNY (OS)
He's an extraordinary man,
Arthur. A powerful man. We
had a connection. I was so
beautiful then. We were in love.

Arthur just leans there, listening. He closes his eyes, it's all too much.

PENNY (OS)
He said it was best that we not be
together, because of
appearances. You know, not all
love stories have happy endings.

(hear her crying now)
And, I could never tell anyone
because, well, I signed some
papers, and besides you can
imagine what people would say
about Thomas and me, and, and
what they would say about you.

ARTHUR
(eyes still closed, head leaning against the door)
What? What would they say, Ma?

PENNY (OS)
That I was a whore, and Thomas
Wayne was a fornicator, and
that you're a little, unwanted
bastard.

AND THE BATHROOM DOOR SUDDENLY SWINGS OPEN,
and Arthur falls face first into the bathroom—

Just missing his mother, crashing down onto the floor—

INT. METRO TRAIN (MOVING)—COUNTRYSIDE, OUTSIDE GOTHAM—AFTERNOON

PUSHING PAST ROWS AND ROWS OF WHITE
BUSINESSMEN, many of them reading one of Gotham's two
tabloids. On the cover of one, a detailed sketch of Arthur's
clown face, headlined, "KILLER CLOWN STILL ON THE
LOOSE!"... The other cover screams, "KILL THE RICH—A
NEW MOVEMENT?"...

WE PUSH PAST A "KILLER CLOWN" SKETCH, settle in on
Arthur reading the tabloid.

REVERSE ANGLE BEHIND ARTHUR, see the headline
"Thomas Wayne Announces Run—Response to Troubled
Times", over campaign-style photograph of Thomas Wayne
waving to a crowd standing next to his wife, MARTHA (50s), a
well-preserved former model, and a glimpse of their son,
BRUCE WAYNE (10), hiding behind his father. Only catch half
of his face looking straight into camera, eyes wide, scared by
the crowd.

SUB-HEADLINE READS, "Protest Planned at Wayne Hall Gala." Arthur stares at the family photo.

CLOSE ON WAYNE FAMILY PHOTO, Arthur's fingers ripping it out of the paper—

EXT. WAYNE MANOR, FRONT LAWN—SUNSET

Arthur walks down a small hill alongside an intimidating brick wall, surrounding the estate like a prison. From this angle he's able to peer over the wall, catching a glimpse of an innocent looking TEN-YEAR-OLD BOY tracking him from behind the trees, hiding as he follows.

Arthur comes to the front. A giant, wrought iron gate. We see a long driveway that leads to the big house, surrounded by beautiful trees and plush, green grounds.

Arthur stops.

He sees the boy approach, but not get too close. Arthur reaches into his pocket and pulls out a magic wand—He holds it up for the boy to see.The boy steps up to get a closer look.

Arthur looks over the wand, pretending like he's trying to figure out what it does. He waves the wand over the front gate lock to "try and see" if it will open—It doesn't.

The little boy tentatively walks toward the fence, face like an angel.

Arthur waits until he gets closer and then reaches his hand through the fence and hands the kid his magic wand so he can try and figure out what it does—

The boy takes the wand and it goes limp in his hand before he can wave it—He looks at it, confused. He hands it back to Arthur.

Arthur straightens the wand back out, and reaches in through the fence again so the kid can give it another try.

And again the wand droops in the boy's hand. Disappointed, he gives it back to Arthur—

Arthur examines the wand as if its "broken", stiffens it one last time, crouches down lower, and...

Ta-da! A bouquet of flowers bursts out the end of the wand— Arthur hands the boy the wand bouquet of flowers—

The little boy takes the flowers. Keeps staring at Arthur, not sure what to do or say. Not smiling.

Arthur looks back at him for a moment.

THEN REACHES BOTH HANDS THROUGH THE GATE and firmly takes the little boy's face in his hands—

Uses his thumbs to hook the corners of the boy's mouth and pulls them up into a smile, into a "comedy mask"—

The boy is okay with it, puts his hands on top of Arthur's hands. They look at each other for a beat.

ALFRED (OS)
(shouting)

Bruce!

Arthur lets go. The boy is now smiling on his own—

                    ALFRED (OS)
          Bruce! What are you doing? Get
          away from that man. Little
          Bruce stops smiling, steps back
          from the gate.

Arthur looks up and sees a tired-looking, ALFRED
PENNYWORTH (50s) bounding toward them.

Arthur stands back up.

                  ALFRED (still shouting)
          What are you doing? Who are
          you?

Bruce runs behind Alfred, hiding behind his legs.

                    ARTHUR
          I'm here to see Mr. Wayne—

                    ALFRED
              (interrupting)
          You shouldn't be talking to his
          son. Why did you give him those
          flowers?

Alfred takes the flower-wand away from the kid—

                    ARTHUR
          I, I was just trying to make him
          smile.

He hands it back to Arthur.

                    ALFRED
          Well it's not funny. Do I need to
          call the police?

ARTHUR

No, please. My mother's name is
Penny Fleck. She used to work
here, years ago. Can you tell Mr.
Wayne that I need to see him?

ALFRED

(color drains from his face; beat)
You're her son?

ARTHUR

Did you know her?

Alfred doesn't say anything.

Arthur puts his face right up against the bars, whispers so
the boy can't hear him—

ARTHUR

I know about the two of them.
My mother told me everything.

ALFRED

There's nothing to know. There
is no "them". Your mother was,
was delusional. She was a sick
woman.

ARTHUR

No. No, just let me speak to Mr.
Wayne.

Now Alfred leans in closer to Arthur, almost looks like he
feels some pity for him—

Beat.

ALFRED

Please just go, before you make
a fool of yourself.

ARTHUR
(blurts out)
Thomas Wayne is my father—

Alfred looks at Arthur, and can't help but crack up laughing
at him.

AND ARTHUR REACHES HIS HANDS THROUGH THE BARS
AGAIN AND GRABS HIM. Pulls Alfred in close, trying to
choke him, still holding the wand of flowers in one hand—

AS HE CHOKES ALFRED, Arthur sees little Bruce, wide-eyed
in the shadows, looking out at him in horror.

Arthur stops.

Lets go of Alfred... Takes off running back down the street
away from Wayne Manor, magic wand in hand.

CUT TO:

EXT. THE BRONX, STREETS—NIGHT

ARTHUR'S BACK IN HIS PART OF TOWN, garbage
everywhere here. The neighborhood at night is alive. Loud
kids on the street corners... A drunk seemingly fights no
one... Sirens wailing...

As Arthur approaches his building, he sees AN AMBULANCE
PARKED in front. Lights flashing. Hit with a sense of dread,
he runs toward the building—

EXT. STREET, APARTMENT BUILDING—NIGHT

A SMALL CROWD OF GAWKERS have gathered around watching the drama unfold. Shouting and laughing, loud dance music blaring out an open window, feels like an impromptu block party.

ARTHUR RUNS UP, SEES TWO PARAMEDICS wheeling his unconscious mother down the front steps on a stretcher.

FROM ABOVE, Arthur pushing through the crowd, rushes to his mother's side—

> ARTHUR
> (following as they wheel her, leaning over stretcher)
> Mom? Mom, what happened?

> PARAMEDIC #1
> Sir. Please step back.

> ARTHUR
> What happened to her?

> PARAMEDIC #1
> Who are you?

> ARTHUR
> I'm her son.

> PARAMEDIC #1
> Oh, great. You can probably
> help us out inside. We don't
> know what happened yet.

Arthur follows them as they load Penny into the ambulance.

INT. CITY AMBULANCE, BACK (PARKED)—MINUTES LATER

Arthur watches as the two paramedics work on his mother, descending on her like vampires, shouting instructions to each other while checking her vitals (pulse, pupils), shouting questions at him as they begin to intubate her—

> PARAMEDIC #1
> Does your mother take any
> medications?

Arthur doesn't answer, just watches in horror.

> PARAMEDIC #1
> Sir. Is your mother on any
> medications?!

> ARTHUR
> No.

> PARAMEDIC #2
> When was the last time you
> spoke to her?

> ARTHUR
> I don't know.

The ambulance starts to pull away.

> PARAMEDIC #2
> Does she have any medical
> history?

Arthur doesn't answer.

EXT. CITY HOSPITAL, EMERGENCY ROOM—NIGHT

Arthur sitting on a bench waiting outside the bustling
emergency room of a massive city hospital. He watches the
sick and dying being rushed through the glass doors.
Opening and closing. This happens in the background
throughout the scene.

The two detectives walk up to Arthur, interrupting him
watching the doors. Gotham police detectives, GARRITY
(50s), grey hair, and BURKE (30s), his partner.

> DET. GARRITY
> Mr. Fleck, sorry to bother you,
> I'm Detective Garrity, this is my
> partner Detective Burke.

Arthur looks up at them. Doesn't say anything.

> DET. GARRITY
> We had a few questions for you,
> but you weren't home. So we
> spoke to your mother.

> ARTHUR
> What did you say to her? Did
> you do this?

> DET. GARRITY
> What? No. We just asked her
> some questions and she started
> getting hysterical—
> hyperventilating, trouble
> speaking—then she collapsed.
> Hit her head pretty hard.

                    ARTHUR
          Yeah, the doctor said she had a
          stroke.

Beat.

                    DET. GARRITY
          Sorry to hear about that. But
          like I said, we still have some
          questions for you. They're about
          the subway killings that
          happened last week. You've
          heard about them, right?

                    ARTHUR
          Yeah. It's horrible.

                    DET. GARRITY
              (reading over his notes)
          Right. So we spoke to your boss
          at, uhh, Ha-Ha's. He said you
          were fired that day—fired for
          bringing a gun into the
          children's hospital.

                    ARTHUR
          It was a prop. It's part of my act.
          I'm a party clown.

                    DET. BURKE
          All right. So why were you
          fired?

                    ARTHUR
          They said I wasn't funny
          enough.

Can you imagine that?

> (he stands)
> Now, if you don't mind, I need to
> go take care of my mother.

The detectives share another look.

Detective Burke steps close to him, holds up the card that
Arthur handed him—

> DET. BURKE
> Your boss also gave us one of
> your cards. This condition of
> yours, the laughing, is it real or
> some sort of a clown thing?

> ARTHUR
> *A clown thing?*

> DET. BURKE
> Yeah, I mean—is it part of your
> act?

> ARTHUR
> What do you think?

And Arthur walks away—heads for the sliding glass doors.
Only the motion detector doesn't engage—

AND HE SLAMS RIGHT INTO THE GLASS DOOR. HARD.He
bounces back.

> CUT TO:

INT. HOSPITAL ROOM (SHARED), CITY HOSPITAL—NIGHT

PENNY LIES IN BED UNCONSCIOUS, HOOKED UP TO
MACHINES.

Arthur sits bedside, distraught. Sophie is next to him...
rubbing his back.

> SOPHIE
> She's gonna be okay.

He just nods. Lost in thought. After a beat...

> SOPHIE
> I'm going to get some coffee?
> You want one?

He nods again. As Sophie walks out, we HEAR MURRAY
FRANKLIN from the TV set bolted high up on the wall.

> MURRAY FRANKLIN (ON TV)
> So I told my youngest son, Billy,
> you know, the new one, the 'not
> so bright' one,—

CLOSE ON TV, Murray is in the middle of doing his
monologue.

> MURRAY FRANKLIN (ON TV)
> (laughter)
> I told him that the garbage strike
> is still going on. And he says,
> and I'm not kidding, Billy says,
> "So where are we gonna get all
> our garbage from?"

Murray Franklin cracks up at his own joke. Studio audience
laughs.

Arthur glances over at his mother, laughing over the sounds of her labored breath.

He looks back up at the television.

> **MURRAY FRANKLIN (ON TV)**
> And finally, in a world where
> everyone thinks they could do
> my job, we got this videotape
> from the Gotham Comedy Club.
> Here's a guy who thinks if you
> just keep laughing, it'll
> somehow make you funny.
> Check out this joker.

EXTREME CLOSE ON TV, GRAINY VIDEO OF ARTHUR'S STAND-UP PERFORMANCE. Arthur on stage smiling behind the microphone, under the harsh spotlight.

Arthur watching himself on TV, his jaw drops—

> **ARTHUR (ON TV)**
> (trying to stop himself from laughing)
> —good evening, hello.
>
> (deep breath; trying to stop laughing)
> Good to be here.
>
> (keeps cracking up)
> I, I hated school as a kid. But my
> mother would always say,—
>
> (bad imitation of his mom, still laughing)
> "You should enjoy it. One day
> you'll have to work for a living."
>
> (laughs)

"No I won't, Ma. I'm gonna be a comedian!"

Back to Murray Franklin shaking his head, trying not to laugh.

> MURRAY FRANKLIN (ON TV)
> You should have listened to
> your mother. The studio
> audience erupts into laughter.

ANGLE ON ARTHUR, watching Murray Franklin make fun of him on TV. He gets up and starts walking toward the TV set as if in a trance. Unsure if this is really happening.

> MURRAY FRANKLIN (ON TV)
> One more, Bobby. Let's see one
> more. I love this guy.

Another moment of Arthur at the comedy club plays—

> ARTHUR (ON TV)
> It's funny, when I was a little
> boy and told people I wanted
> to be a comedian, everyone
> laughed at me.
>
> (opens his arms like a big shot)
> Well no one is laughing now.

Dead silence. Nobody is laughing. Not even him.

CUT BACK CLOSE ON MURRAY FRANKLIN, just shaking his head.

MURRAY FRANKLIN (ON TV)
You can say that again, pal!

Murray cracks up and the studio audience laughs along with him. Shot of Barry O'Donnell laughing too.

CLOSE ON ARTHUR, looking up at the television, hearing them all laughing at him.

CUT TO:

INT. MOM'S APARTMENT, BEDROOM—NIGHT

FROM ABOVE, looking down on Arthur hunched over, lying on his side in his mother's bed, his left arm below frame—hard to tell if he's in pain or beating off.

He reaches out his right arm to where his mother slept, the TV's blue light flickering, Eleven O'Clock News turned up—

NEWS ANCHOR (ON TV)
The anger and resentment that's been building in the city for weeks seems close to exploding. Protesters, many dressed as clowns, took to the streets today in one of several planned demonstrations taking on the city's elite. Including a massive rally outside tomorrow night's benefit at Wayne Hall.

CLOSE ON ARTHUR, quickly turning and sitting up in bed when he hears what's on the television—

ANGLE ON TELEVISION, a crowd of protesters, a few wearing Arthur's clown mask are being interviewed.

> "CLOWN" PROTESTER #1 (ON TV)
> It's gonna show 'em that they can't ignore us. Our voices need to be heard. We're not—

> "CLOWN" PROTESTER #2 (ON TV)
> (interrupts; screaming into camera)
> [Beep] the rich, [beep] the politicians, [beep] the whites, [beep] the blacks, [beep] Thomas Wayne, [beep] the whole system. That's what this is [beeping] about!

ANGLE ON ARTHUR, moving down to the edge of the bed, gun on the nightstand behind him, leaning forward closer toward the flickering screen to make sure he's seeing what he's seeing—Thomas Wayne now being interviewed on the plaza in front of Wayne Tower—"...had no comment on the upcoming rally."

> THOMAS WAYNE (ON TV)
> Well what I will say is, there's something wrong with those people. I'm here to help them. I want to lift them out of poverty, help make their lives better. *That's* why I'm running. They may not realize it, but I'm their only hope.

                                        CUT TO:

INT. WAYNE HALL, THEATER—CENTER FOR PERFORMING ARTS—DUSK

ANGLE ON MOVIE SCREEN PLAYING "MODERN TIMES", FACE OF A ROMAN NUMERAL CLOCK FILLS THE FRAME, and up fades the forward...

"Modern Times". A story of industry, of individual enterprise —humanity crusading in the pursuit of happiness.

And as the screen fades to black, we pull out to reveal the Gotham Philharmonic playing Chaplin's silent movie score in front of a black-tie high society crowd... Behind them, on screen, glimpse the opening shot of a crowded herd of sheep, a lone black sheep caught in the middle, dissolving into a mass of crowded workers rushing out of a subway station.

EXT. CENTER FOR PERFORMING ARTS, WAYNE HALL—DUSK

ARTHUR ALL ALONE HEADING TOWARD AN ANGRY MOB in front of the Center for Performing Arts. Night falling. Storm clouds gathering.

ANGLE ON THE CROWD OF PROTESTERS SCREAMING AND SHOUTING IN FRONT OF WAYNE HALL, behind steel barricades. Many wearing Arthur's "clown face" mask... A few wave homemade signs, "CLOWN FOR MAYOR"... "KILL THE RICH"... "MR. WAYNE, AM I A CLOWN?"

A LINE OF POLICEMEN AND SECURITY GUARDS stand between the crowd and the lit-up white marble building.

Arthur pauses and watches the crowd for a moment.

EXT. WAYNE HALL, FRONT ENTRANCE—DUSK

A FIGHT BREAKS OUT between a "clown" masked protester and two cops. The crowd goes crazy, pushing through the barricades toward the building. Distant thunder rumbling. The police and Wayne Hall Security fight to keep them out—

Amidst all the chaos, we glimpse Arthur slipping into the building unnoticed—

INT. LOBBY, WAYNE HALL—NIGHT

Arthur walks through the massive multilevel lobby. It's completely empty since the performance has already begun and whatever security was available is outside helping the police deal with the protesters. He looks up in awe at the crystal chandeliers... He's never seen anything this opulent in his entire life.

He starts up the grand staircase to the second floor—

INT. SECOND LEVEL, BALCONY—WAYNE HALL—NIGHT

ARTHUR MAKING HIS WAY THROUGH THE SHADOWS ALONG THE BACK WALL OF THE BALCONY, a birds-eye-view, looking around for Thomas Wayne in the sold-out black-tie audience—

He catches bits of the silent movie projected down on stage behind the orchestra, the Tramp working in a factory.

He continues moving along the back wall looking for Thomas Wayne, sees him sitting in a box seat on the side of the theater with his wife.

Arthur watches him in the darkness, waiting—

INT. BALCONY, SECOND LEVEL—LATER

PROJECTED ON SCREEN, the Tramp roller skating blindfolded on a date with the Gamin (Paulette Goddard) in a department store. Arthur's still standing against the back wall in the shadows, laughing along with the rest of the audience watching the Tramp skate blindfolded, skirting along the edge of a balcony with no rail, orchestra playing the bouncy score.

Arthur's really enjoying the movie, almost forgetting for a moment why he's there, when he glances over to Thomas Wayne's box and sees him leaving, being led by his BODYGUARD—

Arthur's eyes go wide and he quickly turns to go, behind him on screen, the Tramp is rescued by the girl before he falls off the edge, orchestra swelling—

INT. SECOND LEVEL—WAYNE HALL—CONTINUOUS

Arthur catches a glimpse of Thomas Wayne heading into the men's room, his bodyguard waiting by the door, still hear the orchestra playing the score—

Arthur glances around the lobby, sees a lobby broom and upright dustpan tucked in the corner—

INT. HALLWAY, MEN'S ROOM—WAYNE HALL—SECONDS LATER

Arthur's sweeping up the hallway with his head down, hear the orchestra playing the melancholy "Smile" from the film's score. He sweeps along to the music like Emmett Kelly's famous act... Sweeping around the bodyguard's feet...

Annoyed, he moves a bit away from the bathroom door... And doesn't give Arthur a second look as he heads inside...

INT. MEN'S ROOM, WAYNE HALL—CONTINUOUS

Arthur sweeps his way into the cavernous, black-and-white tiled bathroom, ornate gold fixtures. It's empty save for Thomas Wayne peeing at the far end of a long line of urinals.

Arthur takes a deep breath, and walks down the line of urinals right up next to Thomas Wayne—

He stands there for a beat while Thomas urinates, lobby broom and upright dustpan in hand—

> THOMAS WAYNE
> (glances over; annoyed)
> Can I help you, pal?

> ARTHUR
> What? Yeah. No I, I—

> THOMAS WAYNE
> (interrupting)
> You need to get in here or
> something?

Thomas Wayne finishes and zips his fly back up. Arthur is not sure what to say to him, just says—

> ARTHUR
> Dad. It's me.

Beat.

But Thomas Wayne doesn't hear him, he was flushing the urinal. He walks toward the sink.

> THOMAS WAYNE
> Excuse me?

Arthur follows after him.

> ARTHUR
> My name is Arthur. I'm Penny's son.
>
> (beat)
> I, I know everything. And I don't want anything from you. Well... maybe a hug.

And Arthur smiles, it's all very emotional for him. Thomas looks over at him like he's fucking crazy.

> THOMAS WAYNE
> Jesus. You're the guy who came by my house yesterday.

Arthur nods, relieved he finally broke through.

> ARTHUR
> Yes. But they wouldn't let me in, wouldn't let me see you. So I came here. I have so many questions.

Thomas Wayne just laughs to himself and turns on the gold faucets at one of the sinks.

THOMAS WAYNE
Look pal, I'm not your father.

What's wrong with you?

ARTHUR
How do you know?

Thomas Wayne just keeps washing his hands, doesn't even look over at Arthur.

THOMAS WAYNE
Cause you were adopted. And I never slept with your mother. What do you want from me, money?

ARTHUR
No. What? I wasn't adopted.

Thomas starts drying his hands.

THOMAS WAYNE
She never told you? Your mother adopted you *after* she worked for us. She was arrested when you were four years old and committed to Arkham State Hospital. She's batshit crazy.

Arthur starts to smile, feels a laugh coming on.

ARTHUR
No. No, I don't believe that.

Thomas finishes drying his hands. Turns to Arthur, his tone way more serious now.

> **THOMAS WAYNE**
> I don't really give a shit what
> you believe.
>
> (steps in closer)
> But if you ever come to my
> house again, if you ever talk to
> my son again, if I ever even
> <u>hear</u> about you again, I'll—

AND ARTHUR CRACKS UP LAUGHING, interrupting his threat. Laughing right in his face—

> **THOMAS WAYNE**
> *Are you laughing at me?*

Arthur's laughing so hard he can't answer.

THOMAS SHOVES ARTHUR HARD UP AGAINST THE TILED WALL, gripping his neck with one hand. Arthur just cracks up louder, he drops the dustpan and broom—

> **THOMAS WAYNE**
> (shouting)
> You think this is funny?

Thomas Wayne's bodyguards bang open the door, rushing into the bathroom when they hear the shouting—

They stop when they see Thomas has Arthur jacked up against the wall.

ARTHUR
(tries shaking his head no; still laughing and choking)
No, no I have a con—

THOMAS WAYNE
(interrupting; raising his voice)
Is this a fucking joke to you?

AND THOMAS WAYNE PUNCHES ARTHUR STRAIGHT IN THE FACE with his free hand, blood spraying from his nose—

INT. BEDROOM, MOM'S APARTMENT—MORNING

Sunshine peeking through bedroom windows. Arthur's eyes are open, he's been awake all night, he still hasn't slept.

Phone starts ringing in the kitchen, he lets the machine pick it up—

SHOW BOOKER (ON MACHINE)
This message is for Arthur Fleck.

My name is Shirley Woods, I work on the Murray Franklin show.

Arthur gets up quickly and heads for the kitchen as the woman continues to leave a message—

INT. KITCHEN, MOM'S APARTMENT—CONTINUOUS

Arthur walks in, listening to the woman on the machine—

SHOW BOOKER (ON MACHINE)
I don't know if you're aware, but Murray played a clip of your

stand-up on the show recently
and we've gotten an *amazing*—

Arthur picks up the phone—

                    ARTHUR
              (into phone; skeptical)
          Who is this?

              SHOW BOOKER (OVER PHONE)
          Hi, this is Shirley Woods from
          Murray Franklin Live. Is this
          Arthur?

                    ARTHUR
                 (into phone)
          Yes.

              SHOW BOOKER (OVER PHONE)
          Hi Arthur. Well, as I was
          saying—we've gotten a lot of
          calls about your clip, amazing
          responses. And, Murray asked
          if I would reach out to see if you
          would come on as his guest. Can
          we set up a day?

PUSH IN ON ARTHUR'S FACE, as it sinks in.

                    ARTHUR
                 (into phone)
          Murray wants me to come on
          the show?

SHOW BOOKER (OVER PHONE)
Yes. Isn't that great? He'd love to
talk to you, maybe do some of
your act. Does that sound good
to you?

As the PUSH IN ON ARTHUR finishes.

EXT. ARKHAM STATE HOSPITAL—MORNING

CUT TO:

A GRAY, BEHEMOTH STATE HOSPITAL looming over the
city block. Metal screens cover steel-framed windows. Arthur
crosses the street toward the building, eyes weary, he hasn't
slept in days.

INT. ARKHAM STATE, HALLWAY—MORNING

ARTHUR WALKS DOWN A LONG HALLWAY, PASSING
TWO GOTHAM CITY COPS AND A PARAMEDIC rolling a
naked sunburned man screaming his head off, handcuffed to
a stretcher underneath a white sheet. Sounds bouncing off
the walls, up and down the halls, working other patients into
fits, screaming back.

**INT. DOCUMENTS & RECORDS OFFICE—BASEMENT HALLWAY,
ARKHAM STATE HOSPITAL—MORNING**

Arthur stands at a service window that looks into the cramped
records office, a metal grate covers most of the window. Harsh
fluorescent lights flicker above. He glances at the hallway
behind him, sees two orderlies walking a dead-eyed patient
back to his ward, hears distant echoing screams.

He's interrupted by a CLERK (40s), ID clipped to his shirt, who's lugging an old heavy file storage box. He drops the box down on a counter beneath the window.

> CLERK
> Sorry for the wait. All our
> records that are 10 years or
> older are stored in the
> basement. You're talking over
> 30 years ago, —I had to do some
> serious digging.

Arthur nods thanks. The clerk looks at Arthur for a moment, like he's trying to place him—

> CLERK
> And, like I said, if it's in here, I'm
> still gonna need a release from
> her. Have we met before?

Arthur shakes his head no.

The clerk opens the file box. Starts digging though it. Arthur watches the orderlies locking the doors behind them, still hears the screams.

> ARTHUR
> Can I ask you a question? How
> does someone wind up in here?
> Have all the people committed
> crimes?

> CLERK
> (going through the files)
> Some have. Some are just crazy

and pose a danger to themselves
or others. Some just got
nowhere else to go.

Beat.

> ARTHUR
> (nods; looks down)
> Yeah, I know how that is.
> Sometimes I don't know what to
> do, y'know, I don't think I can
> take any more of this.

The clerk is half listening as he scans the paper work.

> CLERK
> Yeah, I can't take much more of
> this shit either. Now they
> talking about more layoffs, man,
> we're understaffed as it is. I
> don't know what I'm gonna do.

Arthur looks up at the guy, thinking he's made a connection.

> ARTHUR
> Last time I ended up taking it out
> on some,—people. Bad shit. I
> thought it would bother me but,
> it really hasn't.

The clerk finally looks back at him—

> CLERK
> What's that?

                    ARTHUR
          It's just so hard to try and be
          happy all the time, y'know,
          when everything's going to shit
          all around you.

                    CLERK
               (taken aback; beat)
          Listen, I'm just an
          administrative assistant, like a
          clerk. I file paperwork. I don't
          really know what to tell you, but
          maybe you should see
          someone—they have programs,
          like city services.

                    ARTHUR
               (backtracking)
          Yeah. They cut those. Anyway, I
          was just talking to talk.

The clerk just stares at Arthur—

                    CLERK
               (realizing)
          Wait, I know where I've seen
          you,—You were on Murray
          Franklin the other night,
          weren't you?

                    ARTHUR
               (beat)
          No. I don't know what you're
          talking about.

CLERK
(shrugs, goes back to looking through the files)
Sorry, Murray just killed some
poor guy on TV,—

The clerk shakes his head to himself, finally finds what he was
looking for.

CLERK
(surprised)
Here it is,—Fleck. Penny Fleck.

He pulls out an old file, bulging with yellowing records.
Moves the box to the floor and sits down on his stool behind
the window.

ARTHUR
(saying it out loud for himself to hear)
So she was a patient here.

The guy opens the file. Yellowing pages of her records—

CLERK
(nods, skim-reading)
Uh-huh. Diagnosed by Dr.
Benjamin Stoner... The patient
suffers from delusional
psychosis and narcissistic
personality disorder... Found
guilty of endangering the
welfare of a child—

The clerk stops reading out loud, eyes going wide as he skims
further ahead. Arthur just looks at the guy, waiting to see
what he's gonna say.

                              ARTHUR
          What?

                              CLERK
          You said she's your mother?

Arthur just nods.

                              CLERK
                         (closes the file)
          I'm sorry, I can't. Like I said, I
          can't release this without the
          proper forms. I could get in
          trouble.

                         (closes the file; beat)
          Besides, it's pretty bad.

CLOSE ON ARTHUR, he shakes his head and smiles to himself.

                              ARTHUR
          I can handle bad.

The clerk puts the file down on the counter—

                              CLERK
          Yeah, sorry. If you want these
          records you have to get your
          mom to sign a patient disclosure
          form. I can have someone mail
          you one.

Arthur just stands there, thinking it all over for a moment.
Then reaches in under the metal cage and snatches the file—
The clerk grabs it as well.

They play tug-of-war with the file, it's awkward and goes on way too long. Out-of-nowhere Arthur slams his own head violently against the metal grate, surprising the guy, allowing him to pull the file away—

Arthur takes off running down the hall with it. The clerk watches for a beat, but does nothing.

INT. HALLWAY, ARKHAM STATE HOSPITAL—MORNING

Arthur running down the hallway, files in his hands. Frantic. Unaware he is not being chased. Turns a corner and runs down another long hallway—

Gets to a stairwell door and runs in.

INT. STAIRWELL, ARKHAM STATE HOSPITAL—CONTINUOUS

Bounding up the steps. He stops at a landing above. Looks down, sees no one is chasing after him, just hears the echoing screams and shouts of other patients—

ANGLE ON ARTHUR, catching his breath. He opens the file, flipping through the records, finds the page the clerk was reading. As he reads it over for himself, he HEARS his mother being interviewed for her psychiatric assessment, over 30 years ago.

> YOUNG PENNY (VO)
> He's not adopted—he's Thomas
> Wayne's son. I worked for him, I
> told you, I cleaned his house.

CUT TO:

INT. EMERGENCY INTERVIEW ROOM, ARKHAM STATE HOSPITAL—DAY

A younger PENNY FLECK (mid 20s) is sitting across the table from DR. BENJAMIN STONER (50s), in a dreary small interview room, windows covered with security screens. Penny takes a drag off a cigarette, her face is beaten to shit, nose battered, lip busted up.

Dr. Stoner is going over Penny's thick file, the same file Arthur's holding in his hands.

> DR. STONER
> We went over this, Penny. You adopted him. We have all the paperwork right here.

> YOUNG PENNY
> He had that all made up, so it stayed our secret.

Dr. Stoner doesn't believe her, keeps going through the file, pulls out black-and-white forensic photographs of three-year- old Arthur's body—

> DR. STONER
> You also stood by as one of your boyfriends repeatedly abused your adopted son. And battered you.

Penny exhales smoke.

> YOUNG PENNY
> He didn't do anything to me. Or to my boy. Can I go now, I don't trust hospitals.

Dr. Stoner lays out the photographs in front of Penny—

Penny keeps smoking her cigarette, glances down at the photos, we catch glimpses of various bruises on parts of Arthur's body... A filthy crib... A rope tied to the radiator...

CUT BACK TO:

Arthur looking over the same black-and-white photographs, still HEARS his mother—

> YOUNG PENNY (VO)
> I never heard him crying. Not
> once. He's always been such a
> happy little boy.

> DR. STONER (VO)
> Penny, your son was found tied
> to a radiator in your filthy
> apartment, malnourished, with
> multiple bruises across his body
> and severe trauma to his head.

Arthur looks up from the file when he hears/reads this, turns and looks at Penny's reaction—HE'S NOW IN THE INTERVIEW ROOM WITH THEM, living what he's reading on the page.

He sees his mother lean forward in her chair, glaring at Dr. Stoner—

> YOUNG PENNY
> *That's not true.* My apartment
> wasn't filthy. I keep a clean
> house.

Arthur just stares at his mother.

Dr. Stoner looks at Penny, not sure how to respond to that.

> **DR. STONER**
> (beat)
> And what do you have to say
> about your son?

ANGLE ON PENNY, thinking it over, taking a drag off her cigarette.

> **YOUNG PENNY**
> I'm just glad I got to know him.

Arthur just keeps staring at her as she exhales—

ARTHUR BACK IN THE STAIRWELL LOOKS UP FROM THE
FILE, looks like maybe there's cigarette smoke drifting in
front of his face—

EXT. THE BRONX, STEEP STAIRWAY—NIGHT

IT'S POURING RAIN.

Arthur walks up the long, steep concrete stairway up toward
his building—

INT. APARTMENT BUILDING, ELEVATOR—NIGHT

Soaking wet he enters the elevator and hits the button for his floor. Sensing something, he turns around and "sees" Sophie.

She mimes blowing her head off with her finger—

INT. HALLWAY, APARTMENT BUILDING—CONTINUOUS

Soaking wet, clothes clinging to his body, Arthur exits the elevator and walks toward Sophie's door. He turns doorknob. It's unlocked.

He pushes open the door and heads inside—

INT. SOPHIE'S APARTMENT, LIVING ROOM—CONTINUOUS

Arthur walks into Sophie's apartment, looking around.

He sits down on the couch—

Sophie comes out of her daughter's bedroom, jumps a little on spotting Arthur—

> SOPHIE
> Oh my god! What are you doing
> in here?

Arthur just keeps staring straight ahead.

> SOPHIE
> (beat)
> You're in the wrong apartment.

He turns around finally—

He nods.

                              SOPHIE
                   Your name's Arthur, right? You
                   live down the hall.

                   I really need you to leave. My
                   little girl's sleeping in the other
                   room. Please.

Arthur just stares at her—

                              ARTHUR
                   I had a bad day.

Beat.

                              SOPHIE
                   Can I call someone. Is your
                   mother at home?

PUSH IN ON ARTHUR, looking at her—he raises his fingers to
his head, mimicking a gun.

                                                      CUT TO:

INT. HALLWAY, APARTMENT BUILDING—NIGHT

Arthur walking down the hallway toward his mother's
apartment.

INT. MOM'S APARTMENT, LIVING ROOM—NIGHT

Arthur sits alone on the couch, laughing. The TV is on but
he's not watching it.

He just continues to laugh, rolling onto his side from the joke
that his life seems to be.

INT. CITY HOSPITAL, HOSPITAL ROOM (SHARED)—MORNING

ANGLE ON ARTHUR, leaning forward in a chair, sitting close to his mother in her hospital bed, hear the hum of the machines, the wheezing of the other patient in the room. He's holding onto her hand—Blue curtain pulled around them.

ANGLE ON PENNY, looking back at him holding her hand, still somewhat out of it.

After a moment, Arthur smiles to himself—

> ARTHUR
> Hey Ma, what's my real name?
> Where did I come from?

Penny looks at him confused. Arthur keeps holding her hand in his—

> ARTHUR
> You remember how you used to
> tell me that God gave me this
> laugh for a reason? That, that I
> had a purpose. Laughter and joy,
> that whole thing,—

She looks away, she knows what he's talking about.

> ARTHUR
> HA! It wasn't God, it was you. Or,
> or one of your boyfriends,—Do
> you even know what my real
> name is? Do you know who I
> really am?

She looks away. Her whole body is shaking, overwhelmed with emotion.

ARTHUR

C'mon, Ma, who am I?

She looks back him, struggles to speak—

PENNY

H-h-happ—

ARTHUR

(interrupting; snaps)
Happy?! I'm not happy. I haven't
been happy for one minute of
my entire fucking life.

He lets go of her hand, getting up fast from the chair like a
vampire—

ARTHUR

But you know what's funny?
You know what *really* makes me
laugh?

He reaches behind her, grabs one of her pillows as he leans
down closer, face-to-face with her, smiling wide—

ARTHUR

I used to think my life was
nothing but a tragedy, but now,
now I realize it's all just a
fucking comedy.

**INT. BLUE CURTAIN, HOSPITAL ROOM (SHARED)—
CONTINUOUS**

Other side of the blue divider curtain. We see Arthur's feet
shifting a little.

SLOWLY WE PULL OUT, backing out of the room. Leaving behind whatever Arthur's doing to his mother on the other side of the curtain.

INT. MOM'S APARTMENT, LIVING ROOM—NIGHT

ARTHUR'S STUDYING A VHS TAPE OF "MURRAY FRANKLIN LIVE!", he jots down notes in his worn notebook... Watches as A MOVIE STAR GUEST come out... how he crosses the stage... how he greets Murray... how he waves to the audience.... how he sits down... if he cross his legs or not... studying how to be at ease, <u>how to be a person like other people.</u>

Arthur gets up, adjusting the waist of his pants... Walks across the living room like he's on the show, smiling, waving to the "audience"... He mimes shaking Murray's hand... Mimes unbuttoning his jacket and sits down, legs uncrossed. He smiles and pulls out his worn notebook from his pocket—

> ARTHUR
> You wanna hear a joke, Murray?

He "waits" for Murray to answer. Then Arthur nods okay and opens his notebook—

> ARTHUR
> (reading)
> Okay. Knock-knock.

He "waits" for Murray to answer. Arthur nods okay and crosses his legs—

> ARTHUR
> (re-reading)
> Okay. Knock-knock.

Arthur awkwardly pulls the .38 snub-nosed revolver from the waist of his pants and puts it to his head and pulls the trigger—

ARTHUR
(to himself)
Should I cross or uncross 'em...

Both feel completely unnatural.

Arthur gets up off the couch, shoving the gun back in his pants and walks back across the living room. Does it again... Waves to the "audience"... Mimes shaking Murray's hand... Mimes unbuttoning his coat and sits down... Legs uncrossed.

ARTHUR
Thanks for having me on,
Murray. I can't tell you how
much this means to me, it's been
a life-long dream. Okay I have a
joke for you,—Knock-knock.

Arthur pulls the gun less awkwardly from his pants now, points it at his and head—CLICK.

CUT TO:

INT. MOM'S APARTMENT, BATHROOM—NEXT AFTERNOON

ARTHUR'S LEANING OVER THE BATHROOM SINK, water running. He's wearing rust colored pants and a white "beater" T-shirt. "Rock n' Roll (Part 1)" blaring from a transistor radio.

Arthur lifts his head. He's dyed his hair green like his old clown wig—but he's missed spots. Some of his hair is still its original color, sticking out all helter-skelter.

He does a quick spin to the music, gyrating his hips to the thumping beat—

CUT TO:

INT. MOM'S BEDROOM, APARTMENT—AFTERNOON

Arthur applying his mom's lipstick, outlining his large clown smile, sitting at her vanity in front of the three-way mirror. White grease-paint covering his face. He glances at a mask hanging off the corner of the mirror. He's trying to copy how it looks. <u>A copy of a copy of himself</u>.

He hears someone knocking on the front door—

Arthur opens a small drawer, rummaging around looking for something. Finds some old rusty scissors and pockets them.

Before he closes the drawer, he notices some old photographs of his mother. Sees one that makes him stop. He pulls it out—

ANGLE ON BLACK & WHITE PHOTOGRAPH OF A YOUNG PENNY, laughing at something or someone out of frame. She looks so young and beautiful and happy. Flipping over the photo, sees a handwritten note on the back, "Love your smile—TW"

ANGLE ON ARTHUR, staring at the note on the back as he hears LOUDER BANGING on the door. He glances up at his three reflections in the mirrors—

INT. FRONT DOOR, MOM'S APARTMENT—AFTERNOON

Arthur unlocks the locks, keeping the security chain latched, and cracks open the door,—Sees Randall. Looks down, and sees Gary next to him. Undoes the chain and opens the door for them—

Randall and Gary get a look at Arthur's face, his dyed green hair still wet, streaking white grease-paint smeared over his face, red lips half done—

> GARY
> (re: his look)
> Hey Arthur, how's it going?

> ARTHUR
> Oh hey guys. Come on in.

> GARY
> You get a new gig?

> ARTHUR
> No.

Arthur shakes his head no, steps aside so they can come in, palming the scissors in his hand—

> RANDALL
> You must be goin' down to that
> rally at City Hall, right? I hear
> it's gonna be nuts.

> ARTHUR
> Is that today?

Randall looks at him and laughs—

> RANDALL
> Yeah. What's with the makeup
> then?

Arthur shuts the door behind them. Locks the chain-lock.

> ARTHUR
> My mom died. I'm celebrating.

Randall and Gary share a look... that's weird.

> RANDALL
> (nodding)
> Right, we heard. That's why we
> came by, figured you could use
> some cheering up.

Arthur stares at Randall.

> ARTHUR
> (beat)
> That's sweet. But no, I feel good.
> I stopped taking my medication.
> I feel a lot better now.

RANDALL

Oh, okay. Well, good for you.

(beat)

Listen, I don't know if you heard,
but the cops have been coming
around the shop—talking to all
the guys about those subway
murders. And um—

GARY (interrupting)

They didn't talk to me.

RANDALL

(annoyed)

That's because the suspect was a
regular-sized person. If it was a
fucking midget you'd be in jail
right now.

(back to Arthur, sincere)

Anyway, Hoyt said they talked
to you and now they're looking
for me, and, and I just wanna
know what you said. Make sure
our stories line up, bein' that
you're my boy and all.

ARTHUR

Yeah, that's important. Yeah,
that makes a lot of sense. Thank
you, Randall. Thank you so
much—

AND ARTHUR STABS THE SCISSORS AS DEEP AS HE CAN into Randall's neck. Blood spurts. Randall screams. Gary stumbles back in shock—

> **GARY**
> (screaming)
> What the fuck what the fuck
> WHAT THE FUCK—

Arthur pulls them out and jams them into Randall's eye before he can react. The sound is sickening. Gary's screaming in the background—

Randall blindly fights back, screaming in pain, flailing his arms, his own blood blinding him—

Arthur grabs Randall by the head —all of his pent up rage and frustration pouring out of him —AND SLAMS HIS HEAD AGAINST THE WALL.

AGAIN. And AGAIN. And AGAIN.

Arthur lets go of Randall's head and Randall drops to the ground. Arthur leans back against the wall, out of breath, kind of slides down the wall to the floor—

Sees Gary huddled in the corner, trembling with fear—

> **ARTHUR**
> (catching his breath)
> Do you watch the Murray Franklin show? I'm gonna be on tonight.

Gary doesn't answer. Doesn't move—

ARTHUR
It's okay, Gary. You can go.

Gary backs away toward the door. Arthur sits there for a moment, breathing heavy, wipes Randall's blood off his face—

GARY (OS)
Hey, Art?

Arthur turns, sees Gary at the front door. He points up high to the chain-lock. He can't reach it.

Arthur just shakes his head to himself and gets up to unlock the door.

He walks past Gary who's still trembling almost too afraid to look up at him. Arthur leans over him and undoes the chain, opens the door. Gary takes off, Arthur closing the door behind him—

ANGLE ON ARTHUR, leaning his back against the wall. Takes out a cigarette, lights it with his left hand and smokes.

Exhales deeply.

CUT TO:

INT. MOM'S BEDROOM, APARTMENT—LATE AFTERNOON

(Over the following, we don't see Arthur's face. We don't reveal his finished "look" just yet.)

CLOSE PICKING UP HIS NOTEBOOK, fanning through the pages—

INT. LIVING ROOM, MOM'S APARTMENT—LATE AFTERNOON

CLOSE ON TAKING RANDALL'S WALLET OUT OF HIS BLOOD SOAKED PANTS, pulling out all the cash.

INT. KITCHEN, MOM'S APARTMENT—LATE AFTERNOON

ARTHUR'S POV FINISHING WRITING A NOTE, "...on Murray Franklin Tonight—Pleese Watch!"

CLOSE ON STUFFING THE NOTE AND ALL OF RANDALL'S MONEY into an envelope—

TURNING ENVELOPE OVER, WRITING "SOFI" on the front.

INT. HALLWAY, APARTMENT BUILDING—LATE AFTERNOON

FOLLOWING BEHIND ARTHUR, walking down the hallway as if in slow motion, heading for Sophie's apartment. His dyed green hair now slicked back.

He's wearing an ill-fitting rust-colored suit.

STILL FROM BEHIND, he lays the envelope in front of Sophie's door, then pulls something else out of his pocket— his body obscuring what it is—puts it down by her door and leaves.

As he walks away down the hallway, we see what else Arthur left behind—

HIS MAGIC WAND OF FLOWERS, at Sophie's door.

Hold.

INT. ELEVATOR, HALLWAY—LATE AFTERNOON

FROM BEHIND ARTHUR STEPPING ONTO THE ELEVATOR,
TURNING TO FACE US AS THE DOOR STARTS TO CLOSE,
FINALLY REVEALING HIS LOOK—

Green hair slicked back like one of the Wall Street assholes
he killed... White grease paint smeared over his face... red
nose painted on... blue peaks over and under his eyes... his
mother's red lipstick crudely outlining his smiling mouth...
Under the harsh flickering fluorescent lights, he looks like
an insane version of his mask.

Ding. And as the door closes on his new face, again we HEAR the banging opening of Gary Glitter's "Rock n' Roll" but this time it's "Part 2", the instrumental version—

EXT. STEEP STAIRWAY, TENEMENTS—LATE AFTERNOON

ARTHUR, NOW "JOKER" DANCING HIS WAY DOWN THE LONG STAIRCASE, doing his own Bill "Bojangles" Robinson stair dance... Skipping and twirling down four steps, dancing and singing along to the music in his head (and on the soundtrack)...

...Hopping back three...

...Shuffling on a step for a beat or two or three... Sun setting in the sky.

> DET. BURKE (OS)
> (shouting)
> Hey Arthur, we need to talk!

Joker looks back up the staircase rising above him and sees Garrity and Burke all the way up at the top of the steps.

He dances up a few steps toward the cops..

...Pauses on the edge of a step...

...Teetering on the edge...

Then turns and dances as fast as he can back down the steps and takes off running down the street—

Way up behind him, Burke and Garrity start down the steep staircase after him—

EXT. NEIGHBORHOOD STREET, THE BRONX—CONTINUOUS

Joker running like his hair is on fire past guys hanging out on the sidewalk, glances behind to see if the two cops are chasing after him—

Doesn't see them yet, looks back forward and—

RUNS RIGHT INTO THE BACK of a black guy walking down the street, almost running him over—

THE BLACK GUY TURNS AROUND, HE'S WEARING WHITE FACE "JOKER" MAKEUP.

JOKER TURNS SLOWING DOWN WALKING BACKWARD, staring at the black guy's clown face, but before he can say or do anything, sees Burke and Garrity turning onto the sidewalk from the stairs—

Joker takes off across the street, Burke and Garrity chase after him, "Rock 'n' Roll (Part 2)" still playing—

EXT. SIDE ALLEY, TENEMENTS—CONTINUOUS

Joker cuts through the garbage-filled alley, the usual gang of kids hanging out on their fire escape—

Garrity and Burke run into the alley, the kids on the fire escape start throwing whatever shit they can find at them, hurling insults in Spanish at the cops—

EXT. SIDE ALLEY, JEROME AVE—CONTINUOUS

Joker darts out from the alley onto the busy avenue, the elevated train entrance down across the way on the next corners. Joker runs across the street without looking—

RUNNING RIGHT IN FRONT OF AN ONCOMING YELLOW CAB—

BAM!

The cab hits him and Joker goes crashing into the windshield. Bounces up and over the car. Landing hard on the pavement—

Joker pops back up from getting hit. He's in pain. But not dead.

Burke has drawn his service revolver as he runs out of the alley with Garrity—

Joker takes off running, limping down the street toward the entrance for the elevated train, passing a few other people dressed as clowns, some in "Joker" masks, others painted up to look like the "Joker" mask...

EXT. ELEVATED TRAIN STATION, STEPS—CONTINUOUS

Joker hustling up the stairs, dripping sweat, his white grease-paint running down his face, starts to slow down as he mixes in with the crowd of clowns.

He gets to the top of the stairs, sees the waiting Jerome Ave/Downtown Express Train, looks back and catches a glimpse of Garrity and Burke at the bottom—

EXT. PLATFORM, ELEVATED TRAIN STATION—CONTINUOUS

Joker makes his way down the crowded platform, passengers starting to file on the train. It's packed with protesters heading to the rally at City Hall. Many carrying signs, most of them look like Joker, or are dressed as clowns. Joker fits in with all of them. "Rock 'n' Roll (Part 2)" ends.

Joker looks through the crowd of clowns and sees the two cops getting to the top of the stairs, looking up and down the platform for him. Pulling out their badges on chains from around their necks. Identifying themselves as cops.

Joker's willing the doors to close. But they don't.

The two detectives run onto the train just as the doors are finally closing—

**INT. JEROME AVE/DOWNTOWN EXPRESS (MOVING)—
CONTINUOUS**

Joker moves through the loud train pushing through the
rowdy protesters—Into the next car, all of them packed.

AS THE TRAIN GOES UNDERGROUND, the lights flicker on
and off—car GOING BLACK FOR A FEW SECONDS as the
train turns and dips and speeds down the tracks.

Joker glances back at Burke and Garrity pulling out their
badges on chains around their necks. Smith & Wesson service
revolvers by their sides. Shouting at the crowd, identifying
themselves as cops.

Joker hears some on the train shouting back in anger at the
police, keeps moving... past clown-faced protesters carrying
signs, "RESIST"... "AM I A CLOWN?"... "SAVE A CITY, KILL A
YUPPIE"...

The two cops push through the car, scanning all the "clown"
faces... So many look like Joker. They just shove protesters
out of the way, shouting at them all the while. A few more
voices rising up in protest—

Joker feels Burke and Garrity behind him getting closer. In
the flickering light sees a DRUNK GUY (20s) wearing a 'Joker'
mask and pulls it right off his face—

The drunk guy turns ready to fight.

He throws a punch at Joker, and Joker steps out of the way—
The guy pummels someone else—

A FIGHT BREAKS OUT, spilling down the car.

Joker slips the clown mask over his clown face—

AND JUST STANDS THERE IN THE MIDDLE OF THE CHAOS, at home with the mayhem all around him—

Garrity and Burke spot Joker's rust colored suit in the middle of the unruly mob—

Burke pulls his gun—

> DET. BURKE
> (shouting)
> EVERYBODY DOWN, GOTHAM
> PD!

The crowd doesn't drop to the ground. They just keep fighting with each other—

Burke sees Joker just standing there. Keeps yelling for the crowd to get down, get down, but they don't listen to him—

He starts shoving protesters down, out of the way—and

AND THEN THE MOB TURNS ON HIM AND GARRITY, starts closing in around them—

Garrity and Burke are pointing their guns at the crowd, yelling panicked for them to back off, back off, and one idiot reaches for Garrity's gun—

Bang.

Burke fires into the crowd, as the train pulls into the station—

A protester falls dead. The other clowns on the train go crazy, turning on the cops.

As the subway doors open, the violence spills out onto the platform, catch a glimpse of Joker walking away from the chaos. Taking off the mask and dropping it at his side as he heads up the stairs, disappearing into the crowd.

EXT. NCB STUDIOS, FRANKLIN THEATER—MIDTOWN—DUSK

WIDE SHOT, excited line of ticket holders waiting to get into "Live with Murray Franklin!" The poster marquee box near the door reads: "TONIGHT'S GUESTS. Lance Reynolds. Dr. Sally Friedman. And Special Guest."

INT. STUDIO 4B, STAGE—FRANKLIN THEATER—NIGHT

WIDE SHOT, set for "LIVE WITH MURRAY FRANKLIN!" is dark... but we can still make out his desk... the guest couch... Ellis Drane's bandstand... huge multicolored curtain. Three TV monitors hang from the ceiling, facing the audience seats. Three studio cameras on the floor, black cables strewn everywhere.

INT. HALLWAY, FRANKLIN THEATER—NIGHT

WIDE SHOT, empty hallway.

Then Murray Franklin turns the corner, walking fast toward the drab dressing rooms with his producer, GENE UFLAND (50s), who's holding the show's rundown rolled up in his hand. Murray looks a little more frayed around the edges than he did in Arthur's fantasy.

> GENE UFLAND
> —You gotta see this nut for
> yourself, Murray. I don't think
> we can put him on. With all the
> shit that's going on out there.

MURRAY FRANKLIN
(in a sour mood; annoyed)
Jesus, Gene, I don't have time for
this. Cindy's been breaking my
balls all day.

GENE UFLAND
She's still mad at you about that
thing?

MURRAY FRANKLIN
Four marriages, you'd think I'da
fuckin' learned *something.*

(then)
What do I gotta see? I already
know he's a nut. That's *why* we're
putting him on, it's a goof.

A young BLONDE INTERN walks by in the opposite direction.
She nervously smiles to them and keeps walking. Both men
turn and check out her ass. Murray winks at Gene.

GENE UFLAND
(just shakes his head, and smiles)
I'm telling you, you gotta see
him, Murray. I think it's too
risky, the show's too big. It's
worth too much to blow it on
this,—this freak.

INT. DRESSING ROOM, FRANKLIN THEATER—CONTINUOUS

Joker's sitting on a small couch in the cramped dressing
room, watching the local news on a TV that's mounted up

on the wall, <u>live shots from the subway station where Burke</u> <u>shot the protestor, footage of the City Hall rally, clashes</u> <u>with police.</u>

He's cleaned himself up as best he could... white grease-paint smeared more evenly over his face, green dyed hair slicked back in place. Red lips redone.

Murray and his producer Gene open the dressing room door without knocking—

Joker gets up off the couch and goes to shake Murray's hand. Murray pauses when he sees Joker's face.

> JOKER
> (shakes Murray's hand; effusive)
> Murray,—

> GENE UFLAND
> It's Mr. Franklin, buddy.

> MURRAY FRANKLIN
> Oh shut up, Gene. Who gives a shit.

> JOKER
> Thanks, Murray. I feel like I know you,—I've been watching you forever. My mother never missed a show.

Murray nods not listening, he's heard this before.

> MURRAY FRANKLIN
> So what's with the face? Are you part of the protests?

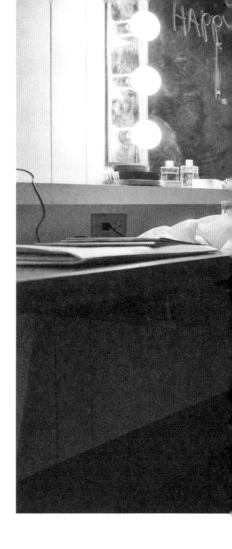

JOKER

No, I don't believe in any of that.
I don't believe in anything. I just
thought it would be good for
my act.

GENE UFLAND
(upset)
Your act? Did you hear what
happened on the subway? Some
clown got killed.

Joker looks like he's about to bust out laughing. All of that news is playing out on the TV behind him. He takes a deep breath. Swallows the laugh.

Beat.

JOKER

No. I hadn't heard.

GENE UFLAND

(turns to Murray)

—the audience is gonna go crazy

if you put him on. It was okay
maybe for a bit, but not a whole
segment.

Murray thinks about it for a beat.

> **MURRAY FRANKLIN**
> No. I think it works. We're
> gonna go with it.

Gene rubs his temples, he doesn't like this, but Murray is
the boss.

JOKER
Thank you, Murray.

MURRAY FRANKLIN
(flashes his bemused smile; condescending)
Couple rules though,—No
cursing, no off-color material, we
do a clean show, okay? You'll be
on after Dr. Sally. Someone will
come and get you. Good?

Joker nods good. Smiles back at Murray.

Murray and Gene turn to go, exchanging smirks with each other as they walk out, making light of Joker who we see behind them still standing there.

                    JOKER
          Hey Murray,—one small thing?
          When you bring me out, can you
          introduce me as "Joker"?

Murray and Gene look back at him.

                GENE UFLAND
          What? You don't want to use
          your real name?

                    JOKER
          Honestly, I don't even know
          what my real name is.

Joker smiles, the guys can't tell if he's kidding or not.

                    JOKER
          Besides, that's what you called
          me on the show, Murray. A
          joker. Remember?

              MURRAY FRANKLIN
          (to Gene; trying not to crack up)
          Did I?

                GENE UFLAND
          I have no idea.

              MURRAY FRANKLIN
          (turns back to Joker)
          Well, if you say so, kid. Joker it is.

Murray starts to laugh at Joker as he closes the dressing room door, shutting it right in his face.

CUT TO:

INT. BACKSTAGE, BEHIND CURTAIN—STUDIO 4B—NIGHT

JOKER'S BACKSTAGE AT THE EDGE OF THE CURTAIN, trying to watch the show through a slim gap. Behind him there's a monitor on a cart playing the live feed.

He moves the curtain aside to get a better look—Glimpses Murray laughing, finishing up talking to noted sex therapist DR. SALLY FRIEDMAN (60s), sitting next to Barry O'Donnell.

>   MURRAY FRANKLIN
>   —I'll try it, but I'm not sure my
>   wife will let me do it. Maybe my
>   next wife.

The audience laughs.

>   MURRAY FRANKLIN
>   (laughs; to Dr. Sally)
>   Will you stick around? You
>   gotta see our next guest for
>   yourself. I'm pretty sure he
>   could use a doctor.

>   DR. SALLY FRIEDMAN
>   Oh. Does he have sexual
>   problems?

>   MURRAY FRANKLIN
>   He looks like he's got a lot of
>   problems. Another big laugh.

> MURRAY FRANKLIN
> (turns, looks into camera)
> Alright folks, don't go
> anywhere. We'll be right back.

APPLAUSE SIGN LIGHTS UP. Everyone claps. Joker keeps watching Murray through the slim gap at the end of the curtain. Hears the FLOOR MANAGER shout, "And we're out. Back in three."

Joker adjusts the gun in the waist of his pants. Takes a deep breath.

INT. DIRECTOR'S BOOTH, STUDIO 4B—NIGHT

Perched one story above the studio. There's a long console where the DIRECTOR sits in front of a gooseneck microphone, looking over a double-bank of monitors.

Sitting next to him are the ASSOCIATE DIRECTOR who times the show, and the TECHNICAL DIRECTOR who operates the board. The monitor showing the live feed is playing a commercial.

> ASSOCIATE DIRECTOR
> Back in 30 seconds.

> DIRECTOR
> Okay, cue the clip. We'll come to
> it straight out of break.

> ASSOCIATE DIRECTOR
> Five... Four... Three...

DIRECTOR
Roll clip. Put up the show
graphic.

ON THE SHOW MONITOR, video of Joker's original stand-up performance comes up with the show's graphic in the lower right of the screen.

INT. TALK SHOW SET, STAGE—STUDIO 4B—CONTINUOUS

ON THE SET, Murray watches the clip on the monitor above his desk, can't help but laugh. Sees the FLOOR MANAGER counting him down silently with her fingers... Three... Two... points to Camera One.

MURRAY FRANKLIN (looking into
camera)
Okay, you may have seen that
clip of our next guest when we
first played it a couple weeks
ago. Now before he comes out, I
just want to say that we're all
heartbroken at what's going on
in the city tonight. But, this is
how he wanted to come out, and
honestly I think we could *all* use
a good laugh. So, please
welcome—Joker.

BEHIND THE SHIMMERING MULTICOLORED CURTAIN, Joker gathers himself, ready for his moment. Doesn't hear his introduction or see a STAGEHAND pull open the curtain for him to go out—

ON SET, THE CURTAIN'S OPEN, Ellis Drane and his Jazz Orchestra are playing Joker on. He doesn't come out. Murray looks over to the empty space in the curtain.

The audience laughs.

BEHIND THE CURTAIN, Joker sees the stagehand motioning for him to go out on stage. Joker starts out, pausing when he takes a step into the bright lights. The stagehand doesn't see him stop, and drops the curtain back on Joker before the audience can really see his face—

Tangling Joker up in the curtain.

The audience keeps laughing thinking it's part of his act. The band keeps playing him on. Joker untangles himself from the curtain and the audience gets a good look at him.

Some continue laughing. A few boo. Most don't know what to make of him.

Joker walks across the stage, forgetting to wave like he practiced. He trips over the riser surrounding the set when he goes to shake Murray's hand. Almost falls on him.

Murray tries not to crack up. The audience laughs. Thinks it's part of Joker's act.

Joker reaches out to hug Dr. Sally as she goes in for a handshake. Another awkward moment. More laughs.

Barry O'Donnell stands there with his hands up, as if to say "what about me?"

Joker ignores him and just sits down next to Murray. Crosses and uncrosses his legs. Can't get comfortable. Murray shakes his head.

MURRAY FRANKLIN

So, ahhh, thanks for coming on the show. But I gotta tell ya, with what happened at City Hall today, I'm sure many of our viewers here, and at home, might find this look of yours in poor taste.

Joker's not listening to Murray. He's mesmerized by all the lights shining on him... all the eyes on him... he doesn't answer Murray.

Nervous laughter from the audience.

MURRAY FRANKLIN

(tries again)
So... can you tell us why you're dressed like this? A lot of protesters are going with this look, right? City seems to be full of clowns these days.

A long uncomfortable beat.

JOKER

(glances at the studio audience; awkward)
Yeah. Isn't it great?

INT. DIRECTOR'S BOOTH, STUDIO 4B—CONTINUOUS

Dead silence in the booth, everybody's just staring at the monitors.

TECHNICAL DIRECTOR

(looks to the director)
This guy's got nothing.

DIRECTOR
(hits the producer's talk button; into the mic)
Gene, what the hell? You wanna
kill this?

INT. TALK SHOW SET, STAGE—CONTINUOUS

Murray glances over at his producer Gene Ufland, who's
sitting off camera on a director's chair by a monitor. Gene
shrugs at him.

MURRAY FRANKLIN
(smiles; trying to save the interview)
So when we talked earlier, you
mentioned that you aren't
political. That this look isn't a
political statement.

JOKER
That's right. I'm not political,
Murray. I'm just trying to make
people laugh.

MURRAY FRANKLIN
(beat; smiles)
How's that goin' for ya?

The studio audience laughs at Joker. Joker doesn't answer
Murray, just smiles to himself.

MURRAY FRANKLIN
(trying not to laugh)
Have you been working on any
new material? Do you want to
tell us a joke now?

The audience claps, egging Joker on to tell a joke. Joker reaches into his jacket pocket and—

Pulls out his worn notebook. Looks through it, sees Bruce Wayne's photo, pauses for a moment then turns the page. Finds the joke—

> JOKER
> (reading)
> Okay. Here's one. Knock-knock.

> MURRAY FRANKLIN
> *And you had to look that up?*

Studio audience laughs.

> JOKER
> (nods; reads it again)
> I want to get it right. Knock-
> knock.

Murray makes a face like, "Okay, I'll go along with this."

> MURRAY FRANKLIN
> Who's there?

Joker looks up from his notebook—Sees the audience looking back at him, waiting for the punchline.

Decides to finish the joke—

> JOKER
> It's the police, ma'am. Your son
> has been hit by a drunk driver.
> He's dead.

A few in the audience groan. A couple even laugh.

Ellis Drane plays "wha-wha-wha-whuuuuh" on his trumpet from the band stand. Barry O'Donnell clears his throat.

> DR. SALLY FRIEDMAN
> Ahhhh! No, no,—You can not joke about that.

> MURRAY FRANKLIN
> (shakes his head; irritated)
> Yeah, that's not funny, that's not the kind of humor we do on this show.

Murray glances over at Gene in the wings. He gives him the "wrap it up" sign.

Beat.

> JOKER
> (just keeps going, on a roll)
> Sorry. It's been a rough few weeks, Murray. Ever since I killed those three Wall Street guys.

Studio audience can't tell if he's joking or not. Murray can't either.

> MURRAY FRANKLIN
> (looks at him confused)
> Okay. I'm waiting for the punchline.

> JOKER
> There is no punchline. It's not
> a joke.

INT. DIRECTOR'S BOOTH, STUDIO 4B—CONTINUOUS

The director stares at the monitor.

> DIRECTOR
> Did he just confess to killing the
> Wall Street Three?

> TECHNICAL DIRECTOR
> (horrified)
> Yeah. I think he did.

> ASSOCIATE DIRECTOR
> (turns to the director, nods)
> He definitely did.

> DIRECTOR
> Jesus Christ.

> (hits the camera talk button, into mic)
> Camera Three, get in close.

ANGLE ON MONITOR, Camera Three slowly zooming in close on Joker's face.

INT. TALK SHOW SET, STAGE—CONTINUOUS

Gene Ufland motions for Murray to kill the interview. Murray shakes his head to himself. This is a big "get," it could be great television.

MURRAY FRANKLIN
(turns back to Joker; with gravitas)
You're serious, aren't you?
You're telling us you killed those
three young men on the subway.
Why should we believe you?

JOKER
(shrugs)
I got nothing left to lose,
Murray. Nothing can hurt me
anymore. This is my fate, my life
is nothing but a comedy.

INT. SOPHIE'S APARTMENT, LIVING ROOM—CONTINUOUS

Sophie's sitting on her couch watching this interview play out
on TV. GiGi's asleep next to her. The open envelope and the
money are lying on the coffee table. No sign of the flowers
anywhere.

MURRAY FRANKLIN (ON TV)
Let me get this straight, you
think killing those guys is
funny?

JOKER (ON TV)
Comedy is sub, subjective, isn't
that what they say? All of you,
the system that knows so much,
you decide what's right or
wrong. What's real or what's
made up. The same way you
decide what's funny or not.

Sophie edges forward on the couch, can almost see a hint of agreement on her face.

INT. TALK SHOW SET, STAGE—STUDIO 4B—CONTINUOUS

Back on set, we can tell by the way Murray's now interviewing Joker, talking to him slower, more thoughtfully, that he thinks this is gonna get him an Emmy... Maybe even a Peabody.

MURRAY FRANKLIN
(beat)
Okay, I think I understand. You
did it to start a movement, to
become a symbol.

JOKER
C'mon, Murray, do I look like
the kind of clown who could
start a movement? I killed those
guys because they were awful.
Everybody's awful these days. It's
enough to make anyone crazy.

MURRAY FRANKLIN
So that's it, huh, you're crazy.
That's your defense for killing
three young men? Because they
were mean to you?

JOKER
No. They couldn't carry a tune to
save their lives.

Some audible groans from the audience.

JOKER

Why is everyone so upset about
these guys? Because Thomas
Wayne went and cried about
them on TV?

MURRAY FRANKLIN

You have a problem with
Thomas Wayne, too?

JOKER

Yeah. I do. Everything comes so
easy for him.

MURRAY FRANKLIN

And what's wrong with that?

JOKER

Have you seen what it's like out
there, Murray? Do you ever
actually leave this studio?
Everybody just yells and
screams at each other. Nobody's
civil anymore. Nobody thinks
what it's like to be the *other guy*.
You think men like Thomas
Wayne ever think what it's like
to be a guy like me? To be
anybody but themselves.

(shaking his head, voice rising)
They don't. They think we'll all
just sit there and take it like
good little boys. That we won't

werewolf and go wild. Well, this
is for all of you out there.

Joker "howls at the moon." It's fucking weird.

> MURRAY FRANKLIN
> So much self-pity, Arthur. You
> sound like you're making
> excuses for killing three young
> men. Not *everybody's* awful.

> JOKER
> You're awful, Murray.

There is no more laughter. The audience is watching this
exchange with full attention.

> MURRAY FRANKLIN
> Me? *How am I awful?*

> JOKER
> Playing my video, inviting me
> on the show,—You just wanted
> to make fun of me. You're just
> like the rest of them, Murray.
> Everything comes too easy for
> you.

> MURRAY FRANKLIN
> (on the spot; defensive)
> You don't know the first thing
> about me, pal. Look what
> happened because of what you
> did, what it led to. There are

riots out there. Two policemen
are in critical condition,
someone was killed today.

> JOKER
> How about another joke,
> Murray?

> MURRAY FRANKLIN
> No, I think we've had enough of
> your jokes—

> JOKER
> What do you get when you cross
> a mentally-ill loner with a
> system that abandons him and
> treats him like trash?

> JOKER
> (pulling the gun)
> I'll tell you what you get. You get
> what you fucking deserve,—

And as Murray Franklin turns, JOKER SHOOTS THE SIDE OF MURRAY'S HEAD OFF—

Blood splatters all over the back of the set. Some spraying in Joker's face. AUDIENCE SCREAMS! Dr. Sally dives for the floor. Barry O'Donnell reaches over her to try and save Murray—

INT. SOPHIE'S APARTMENT, LIVING ROOM—CONTINUOUS

Sophie screams and jumps to her feet horrified! Waking up GiGi who starts to cry when she sees what's on television—

ANGLE ON TELEVISION, Joker gets up and walks right up to the camera. Blood sprayed over his white painted face. Hear the studio audience still screaming, bedlam all around him.

> JOKER (ON TV)
> (looks straight into camera; screams Murray's signature sign off)
> GOOD NIGHT AND ALWAYS REMEMBER,—THAT'S LIFE!

And as Joker waves goodbye to the home audience, a black-and- white "INDIAN-HEAD TEST PATTERN" playing HERB ALPERT's "Spanish Flea" cuts off the show—

"PLEASE STAND BY"

                                                    CUT TO:

INDIAN-HEAD TEST PATTERN IN THE MIDDLE/ BOTTOM HALF OF THE SCREEN... A NEWS BULLETIN SPLIT INTO THE RIGHT/BOTTOM HALF... REST OF THE FRAME BLACK...

A solemn WGC ANCHORMAN (50s) sits behind the news desk. We still hear "Spanish Flea" playing...

> WGC ANCHORMAN
> Good evening. Breaking news,—
> Popular TV talk show host,
> Murray Franklin, was shot dead
> tonight on the live telecast of his
> program by one of his guests.

THE SCREEN SPLITS AGAIN, MIDDLE OF ANOTHER NEWS BROADCAST LEFT/BOTTOM HALF...

Middle of a clip of Joker shooting Murray Franklin on the show, screaming into the camera, then getting tackled down to the ground, hear an IBN ANCHORWOMAN (40s) talking over the video.

> IBN ANCHORWOMAN (VO)
> —the man, who was introduced by Franklin as "Joker", is currently under arrest.

> WGC ANCHORMAN
> (continuing)
> Warning, the following video is graphic and may be disturbing to some of you.

THREE MORE SPLIT SCREENS APPEAR ACROSS THE TOP OF THE BLACK FRAME ONE RIGHT AFTER ANOTHER, LEFT/TOP A REPORTER IN FRONT OF A CROWD AT THE NCB STUDIOS... MIDDLE/TOP RAW FOOTAGE OF THE RIOTING AND LOOTING... AND RIGHT/TOP AN ANC NEWS REPORTER ON THE STREET...

> NCB NEWS REPORTER
> Just minutes ago, police led the suspect handcuffed out of the studio. When asked why he did it, he just laughed and said he didn't understand the question.

> ANC NEWS REPORTER
> (shouting; breathless)
> Looting and rioting have intensified here after the

Franklin shooting. More people
pouring into the streets, many
wearing clown masks. And as
you see, Gotham is burning.

Right/bottom split screen they show the shooting from
multiple angles, slowed-down... Left/bottom they cut to the
IBN Anchorwoman sitting behind the desk... In the middle,
the "Indian-Head Test Pattern" keeps playing...

> **IBN ANCHORWOMAN**
> (continuing)
> The man said he meant no harm.
> Again, Murray Franklin dead
> tonight, killed live on the set of
> his own show.

> **WGC ANCHORMAN (VO)**
> (continuing)
> After he was arrested, he told
> police officials, that he meant
> nothing by it, that it was merely
> just a punchline to a joke.

ALL SIX SPLIT-SCREENS PLAYING AT ONCE, "Spanish Flea"
on a loop, a cacophony of noise, competing video of Joker
shooting Murray interspersed with footage of rioting and
fires, "Indian-Head Test Pattern" the only constant. It's
enough to drive anybody crazy—

CUT TO:

INT. GOTHAM SQUAD CAR (MOVING), GOTHAM STREETS—NIGHT

DEAD SILENCE. JOKER GAZING OUT THE WINDOW, at all
the violence and madness in the city. We only see it in the

reflection of the glass... the fires burning... the mob crowding the streets. Joker's handcuffed in the back of the squad car moving slowly through the rioting, sirens wailing, red lights flashing, blood still splattered on his face.

AND HE STARTS TO LAUGH. It's not his affliction, he just finds it all so hilarious.

> POLICE OFFICER #1 (OS)
> Stop laughing, you freak. This
> isn't funny.

AND JOKER JUST LAUGHS HARDER—

> POLICE OFFICER #2
> (glancing at Joker in the back seat)
> Yeah, the whole fucking city's
> on fire cause of what you did.

JOKER STOPS LAUGHING AND LEANS FORWARD, FACE PRESSED AGAINST THE GRATE—

> JOKER
> I know. Isn't it beautiful.

AND BEFORE THE OFFICERS CAN ANSWER THE SQUAD CAR GETS HIT BY A SCREAMING AMBULANCE SPEEDING LIGHTS FLASHING DOWN A CROSS STREET—

VIOLENTLY CRASHING INTO JOKER'S SIDE, Joker flying like a rag doll crashing against the opposite door, glass spraying—

BOTH COPS BANGING AGAINST THE DASHBOARD AND DOORS, bones breaking, screaming in pain and terror—

THE SQUAD CAR GETS PUSHED INTO ONCOMING TRAFFIC, A yellow cab headed straight for it, swerves right to avoid, clipping the front end of the squad car and flipping onto its side.

THE SQUAD CAR COMES TO A STOP in the middle of all the chaos, ambulance lights still flashing, fires burning—

Nobody inside the wreckage moves. Glass and twisted metal everywhere. Through the broken window looks like TWO MEN IN CLOWN MASKS getting out of the ambulance—

ANGLE ON JOKER, head slumped to the side, face and mouth cut up and bleeding, blood smearing his dyed green hair. He looks dead. And we HEAR the soft and familiar opening to FERRANTE & TEICHER's piano version of "Send in the Clowns"...

SUDDENLY HANDS REACH INTO THE BACK OF THE SQUAD CAR, hands grabbing Joker's body, pulling him out—

CUT TO:

EXT. MOVIE THEATER, STREET—UPTOWN—NIGHT

A LIMOUSINE ON FIRE SLOWLY ROLLS THROUGH FRAME as if in slow- motion, we pan with it to—

A WELL-HEELED CROWD LETTING OUT OF A MOVIE THEATER, coming upon the car on fire, realizing the violence has reached here, the nice part of town...

Gangs of punks wearing clown masks running past, breaking car windows, sirens wailing... Catch a glimpse of the lit-up marquee listing the films playing, "Blow Out" and "Zorro the Gay Blade". Hear "Send in the Clowns" still playing...

FROM BEHIND SEE A SILHOUETTED COUPLE AND THEIR KID hurry down the dark side of the street, ducking into an alley to avoid the chaos—

Catch a glimpse of a punk in a "Joker" mask following after them pulling a gun—

EXT. ALLEY, MOVIE THEATER—CONTINUOUS

FROM BEHIND, FAMILY IN THE SHADOWS see the guy's eyes go wide behind the mask, pointing his gun, music swelling—

> PUNK (shouting)
> Hey Wayne! You get what you
> fucking deserve.

And the punk shoots the man. Reaches out and grabs something off the woman's neck before he shoots her as well. Both fall to the ground dead. Revealing their young son standing behind them—

CLOSE ON EIGHT-YEAR-OLD BRUCE WAYNE, closing his eyes as blood sprays across his face. He opens his eyes and looks up scared at the man in the "Joker" mask who killed his parents, Thomas and Martha Wayne.

CUT BACK TO:

EXT. SQUAD CAR (CRASHED), STREET—NIGHT

FROM ABOVE, JOKER LAID OUT ON THE HOOD, arms spread, his hands uncuffed, a crowd has started to form around the wreckage, checking out his broken body—

ANGLE ON JOKER, A CROOKED SMILE PLASTERED ON HIS FACE, laughing, coughing up blood. The crowd steps back in surprise. Joker stumbles to his feet, standing up on the hood of the car—

Looks out at the city burning all around him... the crowd at his feet stunned that's he's alive... And over it all, Joker HEARS A STUDIO AUDIENCE APPLAUDING...

He raises a hand above his head, does a little dance move and the CROWD GOES CRAZY—

CLOSE ON JOKER, tears in his eyes from all the pain and suffering, still he keeps smiling as he wipes his bloody hand from one cheek across his mouth to his other cheek, smearing a wide blood-soaked smile across his face so they can all see how fucking happy he is—

He is The Joker.

CUT TO BLACK.

A long beat.

HEAR LAUGHTER.

The sound of a man totally cracking up.

FADE IN:

INT. ARKHAM STATE HOSPITAL, INTERVIEW ROOM—MORNING

CLOSE ON JOKER, tears in his eyes from laughing so hard. Still smiling. His head's been shaved, he's wearing white institutional clothes. He looks medicated or maybe even lobotomized.

He's sitting across from an overworked HOSPITAL DOCTOR (50s), African American woman. Somehow it's the exact same room Joker imagined his mother was in some 30 years ago. The room and the doctor also look vaguely similar to the social worker and her office in the opening scene.

The doctor just sits there, waiting for him to stop laughing. A weathered notebook is on the table in front of him. Finally, Joker stops himself.

> HOSPITAL DOCTOR
> What's so funny?

He takes a deep breath, his eyes are glazed over. His voice is scratchy, like he doesn't use it much. But the smile never leaves his crooked lips.

> JOKER
> —just thinking of this joke.

> HOSPITAL DOCTOR
> Do you want to tell it to me?

Beat.

> JOKER
> You wouldn't get it.

The doctor writes something down in her notes.

> HOSPITAL DOCTOR
> How are you feeling?

> JOKER
> Good. Everything's good now.

HOSPITAL DOCTOR
Have you been keeping up with
your journal?

Joker slowly nods.

                    HOSPITAL DOCTOR
Great. Have you been writing
about what happened? About
your episode?

                    JOKER
How I remember it.

                    HOSPITAL DOCTOR
                    (re: the journal)
May I see?

Joker slides his journal across to her. She picks it up and flips
through the pages—

ANGLE ON JOURNAL, blank page after blank page, there's
nothing inside of it.

The doctor looks up at him confused.

Beat.

ANGLE ON JOKER, his smile creeping wider across his face.
And we HEAR the groovy organ opening to FRANK SINATRA's
anthem "That's Life"...

Beat.

INT. HALLWAY, ARKHAM STATE HOSPITAL—MORNING

From behind, see Joker shuffling down the hallway past all the other mental patients, an orderly by his side. Sinatra starts singing...

And Joker does a slide step to the music like he can hear it too... into a skip... and another slide step into a spin... Dancing down the hallway into the sunset...

IRIS OUT:

"That's Life" keeps playing over credits.

TITAN BOOKS

A division of Titan Publishing Group Ltd
144 Southwark Street
London SE1 0UP
www.titanbooks.com

f Find us on Facebook: www.facebook.com/Titanbooks
y Follow us on Twitter: @titanbooks

A CIP catalogue record for this title is available from the British Library.

ISBN: 978-1-80336-384-4

Publisher: Raoul Goff
VP of Licensing and Partnerships: Vanessa Lopez
VP of Creative: Chrissy Kwasnik
VP of Manufacturing: Alix Nicholaeff
VP, Editorial Director: Vicki Jaeger
Interior Design: *tabula rasa* graphic design
Case Design: Lola Villanueva
Editor: Rick Chillot
Editorial Assistant: Harrison Tunggal
Senior Production Editor: Katie Rokakis
Production Manager: Joshua Smith
Senior Production Manager, Subsidiary Rights: Lina s Palma Temena

 ROOTS of PEACE   ⊕ REPLANTED PAPER

Insight Editions, in association with Roots of Peace, will plant two trees
for each tree used in the manufacturing of this book. Roots of Peace is
an internationally renowned humanitarian organization dedicated to
eradicating land mines worldwide and converting war-torn lands into
productive farms and wildlife habitats. Roots of Peace will plant two
million fruit and nut trees in Afghanistan and provide farmers there
with the skills and support necessary for sustainable land use.

Manufactured in China in 2022

10 9 8 7 6 5 4 3 2 1